NAKED PROMISES

NAKED PROMISES

A Chronicle of Everyday Wheeling & Dealing

JEFFREY MILLER

Random House
Toronto

Published in Canada in 1989 by Random House of Canada Limited.

Canadian Cataloguing in Publication Data

Miller, Jeffrey, 1950-
  Naked promises

ISBN 0-394-22078-1

1. Law - Humor. 2. Deals - Humor. I. Title.

K183.M5 1989   340'.02'07   C89-094465-2

JACKET DESIGN: Falcom Design & Communications Inc.
JACKET PHOTOGRAPH: Christopher Campbell

Typeset by Jay Tee Graphics Ltd.
Printed and bound in Canada

This book is for — or rather, in spite of — John McCamus.

Others who have contributed to it, one way or another, include my wife, Phyllis Miller; Michael Fitz-James, publisher and editor of *The Lawyers Weekly*; my hard-working agent, Bella Pomer; my great friend Allan Beezley, barrister and solicitor; my editors, Doug Pepper and Edna Barker; the staff at the Great Library of Osgoode Hall in Toronto, with special mention of my friend John Mackie; David Malahoff of CBC Radio's "Basic Black"; Brian Burns, chief deputy clerk of the Rhode Island Supreme Court, who provided the record of *Manes v. Glass* (Chapter Two); John Mortimer and Horace Rumpole, gentlemen and inspirations; Sir Robert Megarry, whose *Miscellany* books served as a starting point for some of the most interesting material; John Swan and Barry Reiter, whose casebook on contracts has indispensably propped up both me and my computer's printer; and of course those unsung heroes of the jurisprudence, its biographers, the compilers of the law reports.

Contents

Introductory Note

Although *Naked Promises* draws heavily on law reports, it is not a law book. It was written with the general reader firmly in mind, and with the desire to infect that reader with the same bemusement the author feels for our case law as history — a feeling that the law reports are a lively literature with an especially acute angle on the human condition.

The book proceeds by subject matter, and focuses on the human element, how human history has shaped the law of contract (conventional texts often seeming to take the opposite view). One chapter treats contracts made by gamblers, lovers (licit and illicit), family members; others consider contracts made for food, lodging, employment, health care and so on. The idea is to restore to the subject its everyday flesh and blood, its humor, pathos, clamor, musk — to put it in its context of history, culture, psychology, economics and government; to show that it does not exist in some vacuum only those with a law degree can safely enter. "Law," after all, is nothing more than a scary way to describe how we choose to regulate our day-to-day affairs.

Such an approach dictates that there will be some overlap: the principle that retail goods must be "fit for the purposes for which they are purchased" applies equally to fresh crabs (Chapter Three) and vacuum cleaners (Chapter Six). Questions of "consideration" (what is given or got in a bargain) apply to almost every situation, as do, of course, offer and acceptance. Generally, a principle is given fullest treatment when it first crops up; later references lend continuity and tie the principle to its subject and history. Finally, Chapter Eight shows the weave of the subject from Greek and Roman law to our own law today, and illustrates the complications and controversies that persist and still define the subject.

I have tried to avoid "legalisms," although a few are inexpendable. *Contracts*, as used throughout the book, are the promises we really mean to keep, agreements in which we're seriously prepared to give up something to get something. They are part of everything we do, every day, and not restricted to a commercial context.

Tort law was once "a species" of the *criminal law*, and many torts are also crimes — negligence, trespass to property, assault, battery and so on. Where *crimes* are offenses against the entire community or public order, *torts* are part of private law. If Cain batters Abel, Cain can be prosecuted by the state, but he can also be sued by Abel in tort, for money damages. Insofar as tort law holds us responsible for all the harm we do, even if by accident — as when we let a bag of flour rest precariously on a ledge so that it falls on someone's head, or when we leave a sponge in a hernia patient — it is known to law students as "everything Mom warned you about."

The generic term *common law* is used here to mean all judge-made and customary law dating more or less from the time of the Norman Conquest to this day — the law established by judicial precedent, not law passed by politicians. It is "common" in the sense that it is everyday, secular law, and also in the sense that, unless a local government chooses not to follow it, it applies everywhere in the United States and the Commonwealth. A surprising amount of such law remains true to its British roots, even in the independent-minded United States. Some of it has been codified as statute law.

It is not necessary to understand court hierarchies to read this or many other books on legal subjects, but for readers who would like a thumbnail sketch, the lowest courts in Anglo-American law are generally called Police, Magistrate's, City or Provincial Courts. Some have also been known as Courts of Common Pleas, or *Nisi Prius* ("first instance"). During feudal times, when communities were smaller and more isolated, manors had their own courts — as well as their own laws — and the Courts of Piepowder (from the Norman *pied poudre*, "dusty foot," meaning itinerant merchants and buyers) sat only during market times, to deal specifically with market disputes.

Courts of assize, King's or Queen's Bench, district courts, county courts and circuit courts (so named for the fact that judges "rode the circuit" from town to town during the court session, a practise extant in some jurisdictions) can be courts of first instance as well, usually for trials of supposedly graver or more complex matters. These courts often handle appeals from the lower levels.

The same is true of supreme courts, which are not always higher than district or county courts. In Canada, supreme courts are divided into trial (or high court) and appeal divisions, the last being the highest court at the provincial level. In the United States, often the supreme court is genuinely supreme, higher than the court of appeals.

Federal supreme courts are frequently venues of ultimate appeal or last resort. In England, the equivalent is the appellate committee of the House of Lords, which hears appeals from the English Court of Appeal. Until the recent, more "nationalist" past, Canadians, like other members of the Commonwealth, could appeal certain cases from the federal supreme court to the judicial committee of the British Privy Council.

Federal courts try matters under federal control — interstate commerce, admiralty law and so on — while state or provincial courts deal with the rest. Still other courts have more specific jurisdiction — for copyright and trademark or wills, for example. These are usually on a par with district or supreme courts.

CHAPTER ONE

Scoffers and Believers

Pacts with the devil have always appealed to the popular imagination. Humankind's first appearance in the Bible is brought to a climax by a contract with the dark forces. Entire religions are founded on Eve's barter with the serpent. Faust and the sailors who throw themselves to the sirens cannot resist a taste of the same forbidden fruit: the sea nymphs' lethal song promises knowledge of everything past and future on earth; tellingly, they leave out the present, in which the sailor is about to pay for the contract with his life.

The young queen in "Rumpelstiltskin" would trade her first-born for strands of gold, and in Thomas Hardy's *The Mayor of Casterbridge* Michael Henchard barters away his wife and daughter (and thus his soul) when drink gives sway to his pride and disappointment. In Ingmar Bergman's *The Seventh Seal* a knight plays chess with death, spilling the board in an attempt to beat the odds and find meaning in mortality against the Plague; and in the more recent film *Big*, a young teenager nearly loses his soul to a puppet sultan in an arcade machine. The sultan causes him to grow up overnight by giving him the body and influence of a thirty-year-old.*

It is as though we see the earth as one giant marketplace where merchants of good and evil barter for the spark of divinity in each of us.

In one way or another, these deals are an indictment of the materialism at the foundation of our everyday, secular contract, the obverse of our spiritual covenants made with godheads, spiritual covenants that serve as the foundation of our culture: the covenants of Yahweh with Moses on Mount Sinai, Noah after the flood, Abraham in his willingness to sacrifice his son to show his good faith, the understanding between Jesus and his disciples. Where the forces of light would have us sacrifice the flesh for immortality, Satan and his ilk trade in carnality, just as we do, on a less sensual plane, almost every waking minute. Seize the day! Trust in the sensuous! Have faith only in what you can feel, taste, smell, grab!

Yet what is really evil about deals with the devil mirrors what is good about covenants with God: in each case, what is given and received is ultimate. The contract is unimpeachable. It is respected and enforced to the letter; thus the solemnity of oaths, the promise we give to God or (more lately) mortal authority such as governments, and the severe proscriptions in both religious and secular law against profane or false swearing. Oaths of piety to God and oaths in the street with God as witness are extremes of the same continuum, meeting where oath making becomes supplication or prayer. Promises are serious business.

In both religious and secular law, the swearing of oaths has always been legitimate for spiritual and social contracts. Our word *testify* derives from Latin: the Romans, who called their vitals *testis*, sometimes put their hands over their groins when making an oath, swearing on the lives of their progeny, their good names. We swear

---

*In the end, the teenager spends only fifty cents, but not before he gets a lesson in how "soulless" adults can sometimes feel in the material world. The boy's pact with the sultan reverses the usual scheme of adult-devil haggling. In the wife sale in *The Mayor of Casterbridge*, for example, Henchard's motive is to recapture the freedom and adventure of his youth. The sultan, on the other hand, is a "catcher in the rye," a force that can help the teenager maintain his childish innocence even after he has seen the other side — adulthood.

10

by our hearts or lives or Bibles, casting, like the Romans and the Hebrews and other cultures the world over, a "provisional curse" on ourselves, calling down Judgment if we prove false to our promise. In history, giving one's word was no frivolous thing, especially in times when relatively few could read or write.

More lately, what the Greeks and Romans held sacrosanct became our euphemisms. To avoid blasphemy we swore on the pagan gods — "By Jupiter!" "By Jove!" We finessed our own deity, swore to Him and on Him, invoked Him, without calling Him by name. "Gosh darn it!" "To heck with you!" Crossing the line was so thrilling that when Shaw's *Pygmalion* was first staged in London, the theater was jammed in anticipation of a single moment — when Eliza pronounced the word *bloody*, swearing on God's blood, or, as another etymology has it, by Our Lady.

Under biblical law, blasphemers had been stoned to death. God was the heart of the social contract. Monotheism held the culture together under one irrevocable idea, and denigration of that idea attracted the ultimate answer. Frivolous oath making on a lower plane attracted a fine. Violators were required to sacrifice one of their animals, perhaps as a warning that their own souls were in mercy. Probably feeling a need for something more germane and heartfelt, Christians sometimes swore by the saints.

It is an animistic theme common to our folk and fairy tales that we control a force by speaking its name. The girl in "Rumpelstiltskin" is able to snatch her soul from the brink by naming the dwarfish dark force. In some quarters, the proscription against taking God's name in vain carries the corollary that if we speak the word *Yahweh* ("Jehovah") we will suffer a horrible end, possibly without hope of our soul's restoration. The hidden message is that if we make the core of the social contract common currency, a *vulgarity*, we devalue it. Ultimately, we risk a return to chaos. In Jewish prayer, the symbols for *Yahweh* are pronounced *Adonai*, linguistically related to Adonis, the dying god who preceded Jesus in the collective unconscious. Even then, precautions are often taken. When God is discussed outside of prayer, the word *Adonai* is not used; instead the speaker refers to *Adoshem*. Among the most self-consciously pious, Hebrew is taken to be so sacred that it must be preserved only for prayer. As one old Jewish saw has it, in the life beyond, Moses speaks Hebrew on the Sabbath but Yiddish on weekdays.

11

As mortal delegates of the godhead, governments have picked up both totem and taboo. In early European history, kings and law courts claimed divine inspiration. Judges were clerics. (In the Commonwealth, higher court judges are still called "your lordship.") The most common form of oath taking for legal purposes of every sort remains swearing on the Bible, or at least "so help you God." The social contract thereby becomes a double-edged sword: you're damned if you lie, and you might be collared for perjury or swearing false oaths by mortal authority, to boot.

Democracy has inspired ungodly alternatives, of course. If you are not a Jewish or Christian believer, the law permits you to affirm that you will tell the truth or uphold your office, and imposes strictly secular (and fleshly) penalties if you don't. In 1902, in place of the usual oath for court witnesses, the supreme court of British Columbia accepted a Canton "chicken oath," there being a large settlement of Chinese in that province, imported with extravagant promises, then put to work building the railroad. The witness signed a written oath swearing that if his testimony were false, he would die in the street and "forever suffer adversity, and all my offspring be exterminated." East was meeting west in the matter of *testis*. Then the court and jury accompanied the witness outdoors, where he lit punk sticks and candles, slew a cock and burned the oath in a candle flame.

Two years later, that same court accepted a Chinese "paper oath," in which an old man jailed for perjury was permitted to burn a handwritten pledge that he would "tell the truth, the whole truth, and nothing but the truth or his soul would burn up as the paper had burned." Yet in that same province, in this decade, a man was fired from a civil service job for standing on similar democratic principles, refusing to swear allegiance to the Queen.

Just last year, a district court in Houston, Texas, allowed a Nigerian man to give evidence under Yoruba tribal customs. The man, accused of battering his lover with a pipe, swore on an *akomologbon*, a large gourd filled with tribal medicines, that a member of the Yoruba's ancestral rivals, the Ibo tribe, had beaten the woman. Although Yoruba belief holds that anyone lying after swearing such an oath will be in mortal danger, might die in seventy-seven days, the court found the man guilty and ordered him to pay the woman for losses caused by the beating. On the other hand, an Illinois circuit court refused to order witnesses in another battery prosecution to drink rooster blood as an arbiter of God's truth. A Laotian father and son were accused of beating a motorist with a metal bar after the motorist had blown his horn at them for blocking an expressway ramp with their car. They explained to the court through an interpreter that liars would sicken or die after drinking the cock's blood. In convicting the men without recourse to the drink, Judge Michael Jordan ordered them to make restitution and attempt to acculturate by taking English lessons.

Criminal codes across the Anglo-American legal system contain many proscriptions against swearing false oaths in legal or quasilegal settings, as well as against swearing or cursing in the broad sense — promulgating obscenity, blaspheming, or, as the Canadian Criminal Code says, disturbing the peace by "swearing, singing or using insulting or obscene language." In the eighteenth century, William Blackstone claimed ecclesiastical roots for such legislation: because English law and government are founded in Christianity, profane swearing is subversive and seditious. Swearing, Blackstone suggested, was an offense against the social contract as well as the spiritual contract at its foundation, the allegiance to the One Deity. Specifically, this was his rationale for the 1745 "Act more effectually to prevent cursing and swearing," one of a series of English statutes that codified the conventional practice of punishing the more banal sorts of profane swearing by rank. The working classes — laborers, sailors and soldiers — were customarily fined one shilling per offense, which was supposed to be applied to charity. Anyone "under the degree of gentleman" was fined two shillings, while gentlemen and their "betters" paid five shillings per oath. Thus, when in the pages of *Uncommon Law*, Albert Haddock is fined at the gentlemen's rate for uttering more than four hundred curses on the golf course, he pleads excess punishment on the ground that when he is playing golf he is not a gentleman.

Such technicalities were occasionally seriously litigated. At law (and under the social contract), a gentleman was of "gentle birth" and comfortable means, but he was decidedly *not* of the gentry. The gentry began at esquire, just below knight. Thus, in 1718 a man named Brough admitted to being no more than a gentleman when he was sued under the rubric "Esquire, Mayor of Hendon." Insofar as the issue before the court was whether Hendon was in fact mayor (and therefore automatically esquire by virtue of his office), the court allowed the suit to proceed.

Jeux de mots of this sort became a fairly common tactic, as where a man sued on a debt in 1703 as "Edward Nash, gentleman." The defendant, Battersby, answered that Nash was no gentleman, so his writ was no good. When Nash demurred — the legal equivalent of refusing to dignify a statement with a response — the court threw the case out because, by demurring, he was as good as admitting he wasn't a gentleman when he was one! Battersby got off without paying, temporarily anyway, on a technicality. Today we think a "gentlemen's agreement" is one of such trust that it can be closed with a handshake; in the 1700s this sort of contract could be signed and sealed, but still not worth the paper it was written on.

Before the Norman Conquest, profane swearers risked having their tongues cut out. The Normans introduced the ranking system and Henry I first set it down on the statute books: a duke was tagged forty shillings per offense, a yeoman three shillings four pence, and a page, having no assets, was whipped. In Scotland under James I, anyone who couldn't afford the fines was "to be set in the Stocks if above twelve years old, if under that Age he is to be whip'd by the Constable, or by the Parent, or Master if present." Under Cromwell, the fines more than tripled, even for oaths that had been common on the stage at the Globe theater before the Puritans had burned it down — oaths as mild as "upon my life" or "by my troth." Loose tongues were branded. In 1649, a quartermaster was dishonorably discharged for "uttering impious expressions," but not before his tongue was bored with a hot iron and his sword was broken over his head.

Then again, as late as the nineteenth century, a court transported a lawyer to Australia for administering a false oath, even though it was sworn on an account book instead of the Bible. It would be stretching it, however, to say that this proved Mammon had completely subjugated Yahweh in the law courts. The real issue was not profanity, *per se*, but what the "false oath" was in aid of: the accused attorney, William Brodribb, had organized a group of sixteen poachers and administered the oath to them, holding one corner of the account book while three of his accomplices, in black face and carrying sticks or guns, held the others. He ordered the men to swear that "you shall not peach upon each other of the party, so help you God," then the book was passed around for the others to swear on. One of their number was a preacher, who testified, "I did not add, 'So help you God.' Many of them kissed the book. I was very careful that the book was not a Testament."

Eleven of the poachers were eventually convicted of murdering an assistant game warden; two were hanged and the rest transported for life. For administering the false oath, Brodribb was transported for seven years. As late as eighteen years later, the same sentence was passed against workers swearing an oath of solidarity in an illegal union.

But, of course, there are profane oaths and then there are profane oaths. The permissible sorts — when we swear allegiance to a government, good faith in an affidavit, truthfulness before a mortal tribunal — might be more clearly distinguished as *mundane* oaths. In the development of contract law proper, our worldly law of solemn promises, the move from sacred to mundane has been immensely important, comparable to the day that prehistoric fish hauled itself out of the sea into the fertile earthy muck.

Before the middle of the fourteenth century, a plaintiff could not sue on a promise alone. No matter what damage he had suffered, unless he had performed his part of the deal, he was out of luck. Thus, if Taverner had ordered a hogshead of ale from Brewer and lost all his market-day business when Brewer never delivered, Taverner could not sue: he had not paid for the ale, payment being due on delivery. The only exceptions were documents "signed, sealed, and delivered," a rare device in a day when few were literate.

Even when a plaintiff could sue, the defendant might escape liability if he "waged his law," if, that is, he could find eleven compatriots to swear that his own sworn word was dependable. (Our twelve jurymen are a relic of this practise.) These "compurgators" would not be required to know the first thing about Taverner's dealings with Brewer. They could get Brewer off the hook simply by swearing he was genuinely a man of his word. If he said he never promised Taverner anything, then that was truly the case, by Brewer's say-so.

The deficiencies of this way of doing business in an increasingly commercial world, one where Taverner might strike a deal with a stranger and not just the neighbor he saw every day and whose reputation

he knew, finally began to give way in 1348, when a citizen sued a
ferry man over a horse. The ferryman had agreed to transport the
horse across the River Humber, but the ferry capsized and the poor
animal never made it. Under conventional law, the horse's owner had
no contract remedy: there was no contract under seal, and neither
of the parties had performed his part of the agreement. (The ferryman had not delivered the horse to the other shore, and the plaintiff
had not paid him.) But here was the horseman without his horse.

The horseman took the ferryman to court, which found that the
ferryman had promised to deliver the horse safely to the other shore,
and that he had breached that *implied* promise, which the court called
"assumpsit." In the ensuing years, under the new "writ of assumpsit," a plaintiff could sue on a promise itself, and because eventually
the defendant could no longer "wage his law" in defense, the promise alone, without reference to the piety or Christian dependability
of the parties, had become in a sense sacred.

Taken together, the cases since the Humber Ferryman suit reflect
what experience has made plain: expanding industrialization has
taxed and strained the law of contracts in much the way it has pushed
everything else to the limit. If we are to understand our law as part
of social history, to view our jurisprudence as both an expression of
and reaction to everything else in the culture, we would expect as
much.

But in the cases, the strain is usually expressed euphemistically,
as an attempt to balance public policy and the community good
against the "sanctity" of the individual's contract — a phrase whose
amazing presumption is fundamental: in it, contracts made by mortals *for* mortal concerns take on the sanctity of covenant. There is
no necessary logic that the individual contract should somehow be
"sacred" and "hands-off"; it is "received wisdom." Like God with His
Ten Commandments from the clouds, judges have sent down word
that it is so. In one of the most famous dicta of the common law,
Sir George Jessel goes so far as to insist that the "sanctity of contract"
is of "paramount concern":

It must not be forgotten that you are not to extend arbitrarily those
rules which say that a given contract is void as being against public
policy, because if there is one thing which more than another public

policy requires it is that men of full age and competent understanding shall have the utmost liberty of contracting, and that their contracts when entered into freely and voluntarily shall be held sacred and shall be enforced by Courts of justice. Therefore, you have this paramount public policy to consider — that you are not lightly to interfere with this freedom of contract.

This "paramount public policy" of contractual freedom is otherwise known, of course, as "laissez-faire economics." Often, it has meant little more than that the powerful, the established order, have been free to impose and break agreements at will. Some of us are more free than others. Just last year, John Ruffolo, a salesman, attempted to sue the prime minister of Canada and his political party for breaching their election campaign promises to improve the post office and to avoid entering a free trade accord with the United States. Ruffolo claimed he had voted Tory because of these promises, and that his vote amounted to "valuable consideration" that made the contract binding. Four years later, the free trade deal was on Ronald Reagan's desk, and Canadian postal unions were setting records for work stoppages.

As suits go, Ruffolo's was a literal attempt to enforce the social contract — quirky enough, despite its philosophical merits, that it was never allowed to proceed to trial. A small-claims judge (the plaintiff was claiming damages of ninety dollars) threw it out on a preliminary motion, reasoning that there were "no legal relations between the parties"; that a vote is not valuable consideration; and that there was no "privity," or mutual reliance, between Ruffolo and his government.

"To allow an action in contract, based on promises made during an election," the judge ruled, "would be contrary to public policy and to the concept of representative democracy as we understand it. . . . The rule is that one cannot be heard to say he relied upon a statement so patently ridiculous as to be unbelievable on its face unless he happens to be that special object of the affections of a Court of equity, an idiot."

If this is not deeply cynical, it is a shockingly frank gloss on "public policy": a vote is not something given in expectation that elected representatives will behave in good faith, as they have promised.

Democratically elected governments, the very fount of law, have no legal relationship with their electors, and may change the social contract at whim, and anyone who believes differently is an idiot!

Seldom is popular cynicism about politics given the force of law in this way. If the judge's reasoning is pushed to its logical conclusion, public policy, and the "representative democracy" supposedly at its heart, would allow politicians to promise us anything but do whatever it takes to preserve their own power and privilege.

You might think that as more people could afford more and better goods and services that their "freedom to contract" would broaden proportionately. In the developed world, consumers certainly enjoy more choices than ever before, but choices severely compromised, if not defined for us, by the hugely greater power of those we bargain with — governments and multinational corporations possessing more influence and resources than most countries. Freedom to contract is little more than a legal fiction.

Still, we make scores of contracts nearly every day, and the interplay of law and morality in them remains irresistible. What Robert Graves said of literature, another expression of our impulse to give our world order and meaning, can equally be said of law:

> There is one story and one story only
> That will prove worth your telling —

the story of life trying to make sense of itself.

CHAPTER TWO

Lovers and Sinners

Cases of this kind have always been found to be very difficult to
deal with, beginning with a case said to have been decided about
two centuries and a half ago, where a man going to be married
to an heiress, his horse having cast a shoe on the journey, employed
a blacksmith to replace it, who did the work so unskilfully that
the horse was lamed, and the rider not arriving in time, the lady
married another; and the blacksmith was held liable for the loss
of the marriage.

Justice Willes, *British Columbia Saw-Mill Co. v.*
Nettleship

Nudum pactum ex quo non oritur actio. "The law will not enforce
a naked promise."

At common law, a pledge is naked (or "bare" or "a mere promise")
if unclothed by what the cases call "consideration." Unfortunately,
a student could spend a lifetime searching for a concise definition
of consideration. Six centuries of litigation have bred into it a vaga-
bond character of *ad hoc* application. Generally speaking,

consideration is something given or up in return for something else. It is the mortar, lawyers sometimes like to say, among the bricks of an agreement. When the girl in "Rumpelstiltskin" seeks the dwarf's help in spinning gold from straw, the consideration she pledges is a necklace on the first night, a ring on the second and, at last, her first-born child. In consideration of these, the dwarf saves her life with his alchemy.

It is an obviously valuable deal: instead of beheading the young gold spinner, the king marries her. But the value of some promises is not so tangible, and the law can be hard-nosed about them. To make a contract enforceable among mere mortals, consideration must have some pecuniary or material value; if the contract is broken, there must be some concrete way to make recompense. But the consideration does not have to be large. When Europe first became involved in the spice trade, peppercorns were sometimes used as currency; a pound and a half of pepper could represent a month's wages. Pepper has since figured prominently in the common law, standing for the proposition that a single peppercorn can make a contract binding. In other words, consideration must meet legal definitions (must be "sufficient") but need not seem to be fair exchange ("unadequate") to an outside observer. Assuming for the moment that bartering with human life is legal, a court would refuse to decide whether the "Rumpelstiltskin" girl was worth one hundred rings and necklaces instead of one of each. The folk must make their bargains as best they can; the law supervises only the formal validity of the bargains. Thus the phrase "peppercorn rent" (tenancy for next to nothing) and Sir George Jessel's remark that

> according to English Common Law a creditor might accept anything in satisfaction of his debt except a less amount of money. He might take a horse, or a canary, or a tom tit if he chose, and that was accord and satisfaction [consideration sufficient to satisfy the whole debt, no matter how large]; but, by a most extraordinary peculiarity of English Common Law, he could not take 19s. 6d. [one penny shy of a pound] in the pound; that was *nudum pactum*. Therefore, although the creditor might take a canary, yet, if the debtor did not give him a canary together with his 19s. 6d., there was no accord and satisfaction.

The joke could be carried too far, however, semantics twisted and tugged to breaking, even by practised word jumblers such as judges and lawyers. In the venerable case of *Hookes v. Swaine*, young marrieds sued on an agreement in which the bride's father had promised to give the couple £20 *per annum* — "£20 *by the year*." The father claimed this meant he owed the money within the first year of the marriage, an argument that reminded Justice Twisden of a "nice" case where a judgment obliged Sir William Fish to pay "fifty pounds" to a plaintiff. Following the letter of the law, Fish had dumped fifty pounds of stone at the creditor's table. In any case, Justice Twisden, and the rest of the court, gave judgment for the newlyweds: Papa would owe twenty pounds sterling for every year the marriage survived.

But what of an "immaterial" promise, one not to drink, for example, or to smoke or complain? A Christian might say that in pledging his immortal soul to "avoid all strong liquors for the space of twenty-one years to come" — as Michael Henchard does in Hardy's *Mayor of Casterbridge*, overcome with guilt after having drunkenly sold his wife and child to a sailor at a fair — a man offers God his most valuable possession. Yet, among mortals, a contract is enforceable only if whatever is given or given up has some concrete value (such as the twenty-five cents in *Big*, or, despite John Ruffolo's unsuccessful suit against the Canadian Tories, a citizen's vote). Does giving up drinking, let alone pledging your soul (which is God's anyway, according to some authorities) amount to "sufficient consideration"? When do the trappings of a completely serious promise become transparently nothing?

A case something like Michael Henchard's came before the New York Court of Appeals in 1891. At the golden wedding celebration of his parents in 1869, William Story, apparently in an expansive mood, had made a "proposition" to his nephew and namesake, William II: if young William would refrain from drinking, using tobacco, swearing and playing games for money until he was twenty-one, Uncle would pay him five thousand dollars.

By his twenty-first year, William had already borrowed heavily from his uncle, to finance a partnership with his father that had ended in bankruptcy. Unabashed, on his twenty-first birthday he wrote Uncle William that he had "lived up to the contract to the letter in every sense of the word." Uncle replied that he didn't doubt it, but then, perhaps inspired by the bad loans, sounded a cautionary note. He wanted to keep the money in the bank "on interest" for William, "till I think you are capable of taking care of it." He wrote:

> I would hate very much to have you start out in some adventure that you thought all right and lose this money in one year. The first five thousand dollars that I got together cost me a heap of hard work. You would hardly believe me when I tell you that to obtain this I shoved a jack-plane many a day, butchered three or four years, then came to this city, and after three months' perseverance, I obtained a situation in a grocery store. I opened this store early, closed late, slept in the fourth story of the building in a room 30 by 40 feet, and not a human being in the building but myself. All this I done to live as cheap as I could to save something. . .

Uncle William had clearly rendered sufficient consideration for his assets, but now he was very ill. The doctor had been to see him every day for seventeen days running. He died before turning the money over to William II.

By then, for business reasons, William II had assigned the rights to the five thousand dollars to his wife, who in turn had assigned them to a creditor. When Uncle William's executors refused to pay the creditor, he sued.

Uncle William's executors argued that William II's virtuous pledge was a naked promise: he had undergone no "material change" to keep it. He had given nothing away; he had given nothing up. He had enjoyed a benefit, but he could as easily have experienced such a benefit regardless of the bargain with his uncle. Who was to say he wouldn't have been a clean liver anyway? There was no contract because there was no consideration.

In giving judgment, Justice Alton Parker looked first to English common law. Consideration, that law said, "may consist either in some right, interest, profit, or benefit accruing to the one party, or some forbearance, detriment, loss, or responsibility given, suffered, or undertaken by the other." The value or "adequacy" of what was gained or lost was irrelevant. On such a footing, young William's claim looked pretty strong.

But then the judge looked at *White v. Bluett*, a case from the Exchequer Court of England in 1853, which said a promise to stop nagging your father — forbearing making complaints — was not sufficient consideration for wiping out a debt.

John Bluett's son complained that the other Bluett children had enjoyed more parental beneficence than he had. Recognizing the merit of this gripe, Bluett forgave a loan he made to the son, asking only that Bluett *fils* "shall forever cease to make such complaints."

Baron Pollock, the chief baron of the Exchequer Court, found it "ridiculous" to suppose that a promise not to bore your father could be binding.

> By the argument, a principle is pressed to absurdity, as a bubble is blown until it bursts. . . . A man might [similarly] complain that another person used the public highway more than he ought to do, and that other might say, do not complain, and I will give you five pounds. . . . In reality, there was no consideration whatever. The son had no right to complain, for the father might make what distribution of his property he liked; and the son's abstaining from doing what he had no right to do can be no consideration.

Falling back on the old Latin maxim, Baron Parke tersely agreed:

> If this agreement were good, there would be no such thing as a *nudum pactum*. There is a consideration on one side [the father's side, the consideration being his forgiving the loan], and it is said the consideration on the other side is the agreement itself: if that were so, there could never be a *nudum pactum*.

But in William Story's case, Justice Parker could look to a more recent precedent, one much more sympathetic and closer to home. In 1888, the Kentucky Court of Appeals had given its blessing to a grandson's promise not to chew tobacco or smoke cigars, habits his granny felt wasted money and "if persisted in" would be "attended with pernicious results." In consideration of grandson Albert's abstention from tobacco, Grandmother had been willing to leave him five hundred dollars, and the Kentucky court had held the agreement good.

Like Albert, William Story II had given up a right, the right to enjoy certain perhaps idle but lawful pleasures that would seem inalienable to some points of view. (A man may like to swear, drink, smoke, and gamble whenever and wherever the spirit takes him, after all.) This was a "sufficient detriment," the New York Court of Appeals found, to make the contract binding, and Uncle William's executors were obliged to pay the five thousand dollars to William II's creditor.

In some circumstances, a court will nullify a lawful contract because the very act of enforcing it might encourage the breaking of laws, obstruct justice, restrain trade, or otherwise compromise the social order. Again, the operative principle is occasionally dignified with its own Latin maxim, *Ex turpi causa non oritur actio* — "An action cannot arise out of one's own unlawful conduct." In other words, the courts will not enforce contracts that offend established laws or social mores.

This defense is raised most commonly when some part of the bargain depends on a criminal or quasi-criminal act. Bets, for instance, are clearly contracts, but where wagering is illegal a gambler usually cannot enforce a winning claim in court. Ignoring the fact that almost any business venture is a gamble, the courts have themselves hedged, distinguishing bets — and refusing to enforce them — as "illegal as against public policy."

Where wagering is legal, "public policy" has shown itself remarkably liberal. Among young nobles of the eighteenth century, for example, there seems to have been a game of "running fathers" against one another. In 1771, one young gent named Pigot made such a post-prandial bet on his inheritance: "I promise to pay to the Earl of March 500 guineas, if my father dies before Sir William Codrington." Today, 500 guineas would translate to something like $1100.

Pigot had originally offered the bet to William Codrington, Jr., but even though his father, Sir William, was fifty and old Pigot more than seventy, young Codrington did not much like the odds. Perhaps Sir William was not a very hale landed gent, twenty years the younger or not. In any case, the Earl of March took up the wager instead, in writing: "I promise to pay to Mr. Pigot 1600 guineas, in case Sir William Codrington does not survive Mr. Pigot's father."

Unbeknownst to all, old Pigot had died that very morning in Shropshire. Young Pigot argued that this made the contract void: the wager was contingent on a future event. If his father was dead when the wager was made, how could there be anything to bet on? His lawyer compared the bet to contracts for insuring ships: if the ship were lost at the time of signing, the policy was void unless it explicitly included ships "lost or not lost." That is, ships already lost at the time of making the contract were not automatically insured. By the same token, the lawyer said, the Earl of March could collect only if the wager had specified that old Pigot was now living. "A bet on a dead horse," he somewhat vulgarly added, perhaps getting into the spirit of things, "is no bet."

Lord Mansfield, of the court of King's Bench, held that the contract did not depend on anyone's death, but simply on the promise tht he "who came first to his estate" would help subsidize the other until the other's own ship came in. The issue, a second judge agreed, was "survivorship," not death. Although neither judge clarified how survival means anything outside the context of death, the court upheld a jury's finding that the Earl of March was entitled to five hundred twenty-five pounds.

One of the most profound contradictions of contract law is its pretense of egalitarianism. On the one hand, under the banner of "freedom of contract" it demands that governments and judges stay out of the marketplace as much as possible, even though in most everyday contracts there is nothing even close to "equality of bargaining power" between buyers and sellers — especially today, when multinational corporations have squeezed out most smaller competitors. Besotted with the propaganda of materialism, ordinary North American consumers have bought into the commercial sop that they are "free," that they deliberately make their own choices in the marketplace. At the same time, anyone who has shopped for automobile insurance knows how limited a buyer's "freedom" to contract can be. The availability of even so humble a commodity as soup depends on which manufacturers will purchase advertising and shelf space. By making a god of consumerism, we have surrendered to the old deterministic view of western religion: like Adam and Eve, we have free choice, but only toward an end the godhead has already designed for us.

For the merchant, "equality of bargaining power" is a convenient article of faith, not a reality or practice. In fact, business is in favor of freedom as long as nobody else really has it. While it abhors government meddling in its own dealings, it stentoriously demands law and order — intervention, sometimes to the point of invasion, in all non-commercial areas of private life. Anxious to render its markets as predictable and malleable as possible, it is obsessed with controlling the status quo.

Many jurisdictions have recently passed legislation prohibiting anyone to profit from a crime, both directly, as when stolen money is hidden, and indirectly, as when crooks sell book and movie rights to their life stories. But again, philosophical and semantic difficulties immediately arise. Business practices so often skirt the borders of thievery and plunder that shadiness — the bazaar mentality — is almost conventional, part of an accepted ethic. How square the notion that contracts for sexual favors are illegal with the fact that they are consummated in polite society all the time by another name? (Sometimes we even describe this as "marriage.") In our "democratic" world view, how can the propriety of such transactions depend on the size of one's bank account and what we call what we're doing? Bernard Shaw is said to have asked a dinner companion if she would sleep with him for one million pounds. "Of course," the woman immediately replied. Would she sleep with him for one hundred pounds? "What do you take me for?" the woman spat back. "That, my dear, has already been established," Shaw said. "Now, we're just haggling over price."

If profiting indirectly from crime is illegal, how indirect is "indirect"? What if the negligence of an assembly-line worker at a car factory or the recklessness of its profit-driven managers causes the death of several car buyers? Should the thousands of other workers at the factory be forbidden to profit from the sale of the factory's cars? What if a criminal's heirs profit from the crime, while, beyond feeling the satisfaction that his family is financially secure, the criminal himself doesn't profit at all?

In the days when suicide was a crime everywhere in the Anglo-American world, life-insurance policies sometimes had a "first-year" clause: companies wouldn't pay out if the policyholder killed himself (or sometimes, in the U.S., worked in the armed forces or a saloon!) during the first year the policy was in force, implying that after the first year, *felo de se* might still be illegal, but it was insurable. Soon, courts were asked to rule whether such clauses were enforceable — most dramatically, perhaps, in the case of Major Charles Rowlandson.

For nine years the major had been paying annual premiums of about £3,000 to the Royal Insurance Company, insuring his life for £81,000. The policy had the first-year clause regarding suicide. By 1934, some unfortunate business dealings had left the major £50,000 in debt and unable to meet the insurance-premium schedule. Royal had already extended him several grace periods. The last grace period was to expire on August 3, 1934, at 3:00 P.M., at which time the major's policies, which he had paid tens of thousands of pounds for and which amounted to just enough to pay his debts, would fall void.

At a little before three o'clock on August 3, Major Rowlandson was taking a cab home from his solicitors' offices in Chancery Lane. He told the driver, "When you pass St. James's Palace clock, look at the time and note it." As he drove past the clock, the cabbie heard a shot. It was two or three minutes before three. Major Rowlandson lay dead on the cab floor.

When the insurance company refused to pay policy benefits to the major's estate, the major's niece, the executrix of his will, sued. Her high-profile counsel, Sir William Jowitt, argued that the major had been insane. (Because the suicide would not have been a deliberate act forbidden by criminal law, payment of the insurance benefits would not have contravened public policy.) At the trial, Mr. Justice Swift asked the jury if it wasn't eminently sane of an English gentleman to wish to pay his debts. Indeed, the major's purpose in visiting his solicitors' that morning was to leave them a letter explaining that he understood that by killing himself "technically" he would be defrauding the insurance company, "yet they would not notice a small matter like £50,000 less the loans [they had extended him], whereas it would be a serious matter if the policy monies were not paid for the people who had believed in him and lent him these large sums."

The jury found the major's suicide the calculated act of a sane man, but felt that the huge premiums he had paid over the years entitled his estate to the insurance money. There had been no idea of suicide when the contract was originally made, and, said Justice Swift, where suicide was "impliedly covered [after the first year], the dominant public policy to be observed was that of the sanctity of contract."

The Court of Appeal and the House of Lords did not agree. Lord Macmillan was frank about the conundrum the major's case put the law lords in: if "public policy" said suicides were criminals who should not profit from insurance contracts, "the remarkable result will ensue that the [insurance companies] who are said to have provided the inducement to commit crime [by insuring suicides] will be the only persons to benefit by its commission, for they will retain the premiums." But in reluctantly finding for the insurance company, if against the older, supposedly "paramount" public policy of "freedom to contract," he added "that to increase the estate which a criminal leaves behind him is to benefit him," and itself contrary to public policy.

To come to that ambiguous conclusion, the law lords considered some unusual American precedents. *Northwestern Mutual v. Johnson,* in 1920, had held a clause similar to that in Major Rowlandson's policy to be valid. But the law lords rejected any similarity on the basis that American "public policy" differed from state to state: some states forbade insuring suicides, while others didn't. Yet there remained the stickier American cases, where the policyholder was executed by the state for high crimes.

As far as this writer knows, no lawyer has argued that committing a crime punishable by death is tantamount to committing suicide. But in the 1911 Virginia case of *Northwestern Mutual v. McCue,* the U.S. Supreme Court found suicide cases to be analogous to execution cases.

McCue had regularly paid his premiums before and after he murdered his wife. After the murder, he had made his children beneficiaries of the policy, and it was they who sued once their father was executed and the insurance company refused to pay. Although the policy and the crime evidently had nothing to do with one another, the court found that McCue was under "an implied obligation" to avoid any behavior that would "wrongfully accelerate the maturity of the policy" — including, evidently, shooting his wife. As in the *Pigot* "running fathers" case, the court split linguistic hairs: where *Pigot* said survival was at issue and not a father's death, *McCue* said that Father's death was not the issue, but his crime was; insurance companies could insure against death, but not against crimes leading to execution.

Except in cases of willful ignorance, an illegal contract may still be enforceable if one of the parties is oblivious to its bad character: Farmer hires Russell to deliver some medals to Portsmouth. From the delivery price, Russell can keep back tuppence on the pound as payment for being courier. Russell delivers the goods, but Farmer sues, alleging that Russell has kept more money than what the contract stipulated.

Assuming this is what really happened, it seems a fairly straightforward matter of arithmetic. But then someone alleges that the so-called medals were counterfeit ha'pennies destined for passing off among the seaman of Portsmouth. (The sailors' itinerant character would make it harder to trace the origin of the coins.) And then someone alleges that one of the packages of coins had broken open in the presence of one of Russell's clerks, giving Russell notice that the cargo was illicit.

Clearly, the agreement between Farmer and the man in Portsmouth was illegal, and thus unenforceable. But what of Farmer's agreement with Russell, the courier? At trial, the illegality of the bargain between Farmer and Portsmouth flummoxed Farmer's suit against Russell: the court would not involve itself in illegal transactions, period. Farmer appealed to the Court of Chancery, where the judges found that the deal between Farmer and Russell was distinct from the deal between Farmer and Portsmouth.

Still, as in Major Rowlandson's suicide case, there seemed no way to do justice. A thick fog hung over the issue of whether Russell had known what was really in the packages. If Russell had been ignorant that he was transporting counterfeit goods, arguably his contract with Farmer was legal, meaning that bad-guy Farmer would win. Under that contract, the unwitting courier owed him the money he had kept back.

As Justice Eyre, one of the appeal judges, noted, the courts were in danger here of promulgating a "monstrous doctrine." If a party to an agreement is innocent of its criminal soul, he loses, "but if guilty he shall be free." But then, neither should the plaintiff (the counterfeiter Farmer) "be heard to make a claim in a court of justice founded on a transaction for which he ought to be indicted."

The law reports do not say who eventually emerged victorious, but by the time of the appeal, Justice Eyre was expressing doubts that

courier Russell knew anything shady was going on. The general tone
of the opinions suggest little judicial sympathy for counterfeiter
Farmer. It may have been a matter of justice plumping for the lesser
of two evils.

If Farmer and Russell had been *conspiring* to pass off counterfeit
money, the only court of sensible resort would have been the court
that enforces honor among thieves. But other criminals had sought
the King's justice. In the 1720s, a half century or so before *Farmer*,
a plaintiff named John Everet had told the Court of Exchequer that
his business was dealing in "plate, rings, watches, etc." Without committing anything to paper, he had made defendant Williams a full
partner, and the two of them had agreed to share expenses, including
equestrian outfitting, costs of accommodation, and costs of business
meetings hither and yon in pubs, markets and fairs.

For several months, the partnership ran very smoothly. In Finchley,
for example, the partners "dealt with several gentlemen for divers
watches, rings, swords, canes, hats, cloaks, horses, bridles, saddles,
and other things to the value of £200 and upwards." And in
Blackheath they prevailed upon another gentleman to part with his
horse, saddle, bridle, watch, sword cane, "and other things . . . at
a very cheap rate." Indeed, they met with similar successes across
southern England, but then Williams, according to Everet's complaint
(which was framed in all the conventional legalisms of a breach of
partnership claim), had refused to share the profits equally.

In light of the doctrine of *ex turpi causa*, it might be giving away
the outcome of this suit to report that plaintiff Everet was hanged
as a thief in 1730, Williams in 1727. Everet's "partnership" claim
had of course been dismissed; shortly thereafter, his lawyers were
arrested, cited for contempt and fined fifty pounds each. In 1735,
one of those lawyers, a Mr. Wreathcock, was convicted of robbery
and sentenced to death, but was later reprieved and transported to
Australia.

Moral philosophy, or a state headed by priests, might go so far as
to say that almost any contract for profit, no matter its character,
is immoral as against public policy. As a bulwark of free-market
economies, but also as a product of the Judaeo-Christian moral code,
contract law must somehow square popular morality with the now

more pervasive — and much more popular — forces of materialism. In 1866, Baron Bramwell of the English Court of Exchequer put the dilemma graphically: "If a man were to ask for duelling pistols, and to say: 'I think I shall fight a duel to-morrow,' might not the seller answer: 'I do not want to know your purpose; I have nothing to do with it; that is your business: mine is to sell the pistols, and I look only to the profit of trade.'"

Modern shorthand for this laissez-faire view says "People, not guns, kill people." However you phrase it, the profit motive can become uncomfortable when conscience walks even softly across its turf.

As the betting and insurance cases make clear, the law reflects our culture's ambivalence about morality, about what it is and how it should be enforced. It reflects a conflict between a desire to preserve a moral norm against a felt need to protect every individual's freedom to bargain — or, really, to profit. It pits, in other words, community against individual gain. The interests of Major Rowlandson's niece, as executrix of his estate, must be sacrified to what judges decide is the greater public good — discouraging, or at least not encouraging, suicide. Then again, a court will permit us to wager huge sums on the lifeblood of our own fathers, just as a life-insurance company would hedge its bets on Father's survival, as if they were the turkeys in a shooting match. In such cases, the law does not consider how such gambles can encourage not just suicide but *patricide* — how sons might decide to improve their cash flow by helping indolent nature along a little bit in taking its course.

The ambivalence is especially clear in contract cases whose defendants are prostitutes. In fact, Baron Bramwell's pistol example arises in the so-called "leading" prostitute case, *Pearce v. Brooks*, where a "woman of the town" had refused to pay a premium on a rented carriage when she defaulted on the rent and damaged the vehicle. The law seemed to say that if the carriage owners knew that the prostitute was renting the carriage to pick up johns, *and* knew as well that she would pay for the carriage out of her ill-gotten gains, the contract for its use was illegal, and the carriage owners could not get legal help to make her pay.

This, anyway, was the law as enunciated by one of the most influential judges in Anglo-American history, Edward Law, first Baron Ellenborough. In the 1808 case of *Bowry v. Bennet*, his lordship had ordered a prostitute to pay for clothes she had taken delivery of, his reasoning seeming to be that the woman would not necessarily wear the garments solely in the course of her illicit business. A long line of such disputes had ended in similar victories for the plaintiff-merchants and prostitutes' landlords.

Generally, unless a landlord knew that lodgings would be used exclusively for prostitution, the prostitute tenant had been held liable for her rent. As one judge bluntly put it in the case of a working girl who was a minor, "both an infant and a prostitute must have lodging." In order to stop prostitutes from getting off rent-free, the courts had been obliged to make a chameleon distinction between a prostitute's workplace and residence, forced to assert that her "office" turned back into a residence between clients — as though, if you made your living as a doctor or dentist out of your house, your office there was not really an office. By such reasoning, prostitutes have of course also been held liable for plumbing repairs, phone bills, and the like, even though it could be said that someone providing those services was furthering an illegal enterprise. A prostitute (or a doctor or dentist) may require heat and water even when she isn't on duty.

(On the other hand, a madam can win damages from a landlord who throws her out, even if she rented the rooms under the pretense of using them for a legitimate business — a perfumery, for example, as was the front in an 1854 case. There, the court found that the tenant's lie about the nature of the business had nothing to do with the lease *per se*, and so the landlord could not evict without proper notice.)

And thus, in one widely-quoted 1798 case, while ordering a prostitute to pay a laundry for cleaning flashy dresses as well as men's nightcaps, Justice Buller asked the prostitute's lawyer:

> What do you mean by the expression "clothes used for the purposes of prostitution?" This unfortunate woman must have clean linen, and it is impossible for the court to take into consideration which of these articles were used by the Defendant [the prostitute] to an improper purpose, and which were not.

In its exasperation, the court did not speculate as to what proper purpose a single woman might have for men's nightcaps.

Lord Ellenborough had attempted to mold a two-sided rule from such precedents. In ordering the prostitute in *Bowry v. Bennet* to pay her coutouriere, he held that even if the coutouriere knew of her customer's way of life, the contract was *enforceable* unless the coutouriere also expected to be paid directly from the customer's ill-gotten gains.

From that time until the carriage case nearly sixty years later, Lord Ellenborough's rule had been making judges fidget and fumble: in practice, if prostitutes simply relied on their own turpitude or notoriety, asserting that everything they wished to buy or rent would be paid for by whoring, the rule could make it laughably easy for them to welch on their debts. As in the *Rowlandson* and *Farmer* cases, application of the rule offended not only equity, but logic: a person could assert her own "bad" behavior to heap illegal profit upon immoral profit, and a perfectly innocent seller (or lessor) was forced to bear 100 percent loss.

Then again, sellers and lessors could exploit the rules themselves. While even at law prostitution was accepted as an ineradicable evil (in both Britain and Canada, prostitution itself is not illegal: crimes consist in living off the avails, communicating for the purposes, keeping a brothel, and so on), the idea that anyone should trade with prostitutes and even indirectly encourage their enterprise offended what the judges perceived as public policy. It was too difficult to prove both that the seller/lessor knew that the buyer/renter was engaged in immoral or unlawful enterprise *and* that she would pay out of the tainted proceeds. Sellers could get away with furthering prostitution simply by turning a blind eye: as far as they knew, they would say, Mistress Quickly bought her dresses out of the innkeeping part of her business, not from whore-mongering. So, very carefully professing not to contradict anything the redoutable Lord Ellenborough had declared, the later judges contradicted him anyway, claiming that he had not been making a hard-and-fast rule, but was merely talking about the weight of evidence. If the seller knew that merchandise was to be used exclusively, or at least primarily, for something unlawful, that was enough to render the contract void. If it could be shown that a seller expected to be paid out of ill-gotten gains, this simply added weight to the evidence that he knew the buyer was making the purchase to carry on her evil ways.

Cases in which sex itself is a part of the consideration for the contract are usually more clear-cut. Where prostitution or "living off the avails" is illegal, no cash-for-sex deal would be enforceable. Nor, for that matter, can someone enforce a contract for the sale of a car requiring the buyer to pay with sexual intimacy. In a 1984 Wyoming case, a justice of the peace found it irrelevant that the buyer had already partly paid for a 1970 Pontiac with $100 cash and fifty sex acts.

In times and places that make it illegal for unmarried people to "cohabit," "illicit intercourse" cannot be consideration for a contract ("I will support you if you have sex with me"). Contract law respects the legacy of Eden: one's money (or one's peppercorns) might be dirty, but one's own body is far worse.

The very idea of biology can be legally offensive, depending on the tenor of the times. In a 1918 Rhode Island case, Justice Walter Vincent was so repelled by a contract to sell "adult toy novelties" that he refused to describe the merchandise in his judgment. "To do so," he wrote, "would only serve to extend the knowledge of and give permanency to obscene and indecent devices."

The defendant was the buyer — ultimately, the retailer of the toys. His brief reveals that four lots of "devices" had changed hands — "Bear Charms," "Bull Charms," "Modern Dancers" and "Naked Truth." The first was a disk, suspended in a metal frame, with a bear depicted on either side; when the disk was spun, the bears seemed to copulate. In similar fashion, "Bull Charms" depicted the eponymous animal relieving itself. "Modern Dancers" comprised a metal token covered with a translucent material. When a match was played behind it, the material showed a naked woman doing the "hootchy-kootchy." "The Naked Truth" was a cardboard envelope from which protruded a picture, on cardboard, of a woman's legs. When the cardboard was pulled from the envelope, a mousetrap-style snare was sprung on the puller's hand, and the woman's "chemise" was revealed, printed with the word "Stung."

As far as Justice Vincent was concerned, a deal to sell such novelties was so outrageous that it was unnecessary to cite any authorities for denying the toymaker the $151.61 the retailer owed him. The problem remained, of course, that the welching retailer might already have sold some of the toys and made a one-hundred-percent profit.

But as far as juridical unfairness goes in contracts supposedly having to do with sexual matters, the most astonishing reported instance is *Gardner v. Fulforde*, an upholsterer's suit in 1667 for payment on a "pair of hangings," otherwise described by his lawyer as "gilt skins."

Latin being the language of court pleadings at the time, upholsterer Gardner's lawyer had described the skins in papers filed with the court as "*quatuor pictas pellices Anglise.*" Deadbeat Fulforde's lawyer argued that this meant "four painted whores . . . , for *pellex* signifieth a harlot." Skins, he said, were *pelles*, so Fulforde could keep the hangings without paying for them. Agreeing to provide someone with four painted English whores was illegal, and the contract was therefore unenforceable.

Shockingly, this argument prevailed, an outcome that probably says less about the law of contract than about how the most minor deficiencies in pleadings have sometimes completely hobbled justice. (Sir Robert Megarry reports that, as late as 1849, an action failed because the defendant's middle name was not spelled out, although the initial would have been sufficient had the middle name begun with a vowel.) The court ruled against Gardner, but suggested that he might have a case under a different cause of action, "trover," which was pleaded where a defendant had "wrongfully converted" property to his own use. A few days later, Gardner renewed his suit in trover, only to be told that no matter how he sued, *pelles* was indeed the "proper word, of a proper signification," and "therefore similitude is not sufficient." As precedent, the judge cited a case in which someone had sued for the price of six eggs as "*sex ovium* for *ovorum*, and the plaintiff was thereupon nonsuited."

Justice may be willfully blind; sometimes it's maliciously deaf, as well.

An advertised reward for information leading to the conviction of a criminal is a contractual offer. But to collect the reward money (at least according to the prevailing view in the United States and Australia), you must rely on it from the outset. If you give information to clear your own name, or out of a feeling of civic responsibility, you cannot later claim you relied on the reward offer. You did not "accept the offer" under the terms of contract law; you merely made a gift of the information.

By such reasoning, the English case that normally would establish the law on the subject seems an aberration — which perhaps it genuinely is, by virtue of its facts more than its law. There, Mary Ann Williams claimed the twenty pounds offered by William Cawardine for fingering the murderer of his brother. But although Mary Ann had always known the identity of the killer, she had kept it secret for five months, snitching only after William had beaten her so badly she thought her own days were numbered.

Whether William was actually trying to beat the name out of Mary Ann is not clear from the case report. Apparently feeling a death-bed need to make a clean breast of things, Mary Ann named the murderer and, upon recovering her health, seems to have discovered that if she were to maintain it, the £20 would not go amiss. The Court of King's Bench held unanimously that she had indeed come within the terms of the reward offer; her "deathbed" declaration was a legal acceptance of it.

If there is a legal principle here, it is so nebulous as to fade away every time you think you've fastened on it. You can accept an offer, the case suggests, even if you don't know it exists. Queasy about the ramifications of such a suggestion, but finding *Cawardine* the first hard-and-fast statement of the common law on rewards, later judges and scholars have hedged, arguing that Mary Ann may well have had the reward "in her contemplation" when she named the murderer. The case report does not say otherwise.

Probably the truth would not make such good precedent. The judges may simply have felt pity for Mary Ann, or enmity toward William and his violent ways. They may have ignored sense simply to make him pay.

Where sex is obviously "licit," an implied term, even, of holy matrimony, any number of legal complications arise. When the common law was developing in the ecclesiastical courts during the Middle Ages, "public policy" viewed marriage literally — Adam-and-Eve style — as an absolute union of two identities in one, the man's. That view persisted for about six centuries. "At law," a shopworn maxim had it, "husband and wife are one person, and the husband is that person." In its vestigial Norman French, which hung on into the Renaissance as tenaciously as medieval ideas about the marriage bond, the law called the wife a *feme covert*, a protected or covered woman.

Until the twentieth century, marriage may have secured a woman's future materially, but it also made her a legal appendage of her husband. In most ordinary circumstances, she could not make contracts in her own name. A woman merely *engaged* to be married could be charged with criminal fraud if she disposed of any of her property without first consulting her intended.

A husband might anyway grant his wife some bargaining power, if only to bind her more tightly than the marriage service had, to extraordinary conjugal commitments. The so-called "marriage contract" or "domestic agreement" now enjoying an exuberant vogue usually assumes equality of bargaining power, a supposed requisite in legitimate contracts. But in history, it often was drafted to maintain patriarchal disequilibrium.

When, for instance, William Dagg discovered in 1867 that his girlfriend, Catherine Jeffries, was pregnant by him, he agreed to marry her. The couple had met at a "hydropathic hospital," a clinic offering a German "water cure" then in vogue, where he worked as a porter, she as a cook. Yet William seems to have viewed Catherine as significantly below his station: she was, after all, a girl who *would*. Before solemnizing their marriage, he wrote up an agreement for both of them to sign:

> This is to certify that whereas the undersigned parties do agree that they will marry, and that only to save the female of us from shaming her friends or telling a lie, and that the said marriage shall be no more thought of, except to tell her friends that she is married (unless she should arrive at the following accomplishments — viz., piano, singing, reading, writing, speaking, and deportment); and whereas these said accomplishments have in no way been sought after, much less mastered, therefore the aforesaid marriage shall be and is null and void; and whereas we agree that the male of us shall keep his harmonium in the aforesaid female's sitting room, we agree that it shall be there no more than four months, and that from that time the aforesaid and undersigned shall be free in every respect whatsoever of the aforesaid and undersigned female, as witness our hands this 1st of − −, 1867.

The drafter was clearly a man of pretension, a philandering porter who fancied himself a solicitor, a twister of word and sentiment who somehow conceived that living a lie was preferable to telling one.

A month following the marriage the child was born, after which William paid Catherine two shillings and sixpence per week, but otherwise had nothing to do with her or the baby. He stopped the payments when he discovered Catherine was living with another man, and in 1882, fifteen years after the "wedding," petitioned the English Court of Probate, Divorce and Admiralty for a dissolution of the marriage.

Despite the written "certification," the court refused to let William off the hook. It found that, in fact, there *was* no agreement outside the marriage bond, because Catherine had been in no position to haggle. Her subsequent degradation, the court added, was a direct result of William's failure to provide for and protect her as a husband should: because of *his* behavior, she lacked the resources to improve and support herself as the contract demanded. Surprisingly, the court did not consider the question of whether Catherine really understood the terms of the "agreement," which itself alleged that she was illiterate.

Fifty-six years later, a similarly heavy-handed "agreement" was drawn to secure a wife's absolute fidelity. Under threat of death, eighteen-year-old Estella Blitz had written, as dictated to her:

> I undersigned Estella agree to marry Mohamed on the following conditions: (1) I know well that he is an old-fashioned Egyptian and I know all about the Egyptian habits and character and I promise to follow all these habits and character without any exceptions; (2) I promise not to go out anywhere without my husband; (3) I will never have men or boy friends of me nor ask any man or boy to visit me at home nor see any man or boy outside or have any appointments; (4) I promise not to write to anybody friend of mine in Egypt or anywhere else abroad, man, boy, girl or lady; (5) I promise not to dance with any man or boy at home or at any other home or at any dancing hall in any feast or in any other circumstance; (6) I know well that Mohamed is not rich at all and he can't promise anything except just keeping me comfortably; (7) I confess that I write these conditions with my own wish and without any obligation from any side, and that I am conscious and responsible, and if I break any of these conditions I have to separate,

and have no right to claim any penny from Mohamed at any Court, whether Egyptian or English.

The couple had been married in a registry office in England, but Mohamed then returned to his railway job in Egypt. They had never lived together or consummated the marriage.

When Estella applied for dissolution, the judge, Sir S.O. Henn Collins, did not examine the terms of the "agreement" — that, for example, much of it seemed contrary to public policy by interference with the administration of justice — and remarked that in ninety-nine cases out of one hundred Estella's story would be incredible. But he believed that she had written the document under fear, terror and duress. And of course, as discussed more fully in Chapter Six, contracts signed in such circumstances are *nudum pactum*.

The assumption among humans that the male should be the dominant mate, that man is protector and master, has proven a tenacious one and persists even in this age that styles male supremacy a disadvantage for everyone concerned. From at least the Middle Ages until the end of the nineteenth century, the common folk generally believed that the bond of matrimony accorded a man an implied right to discipline his wife as he would his unruly children. In the late 1700s, courts began holding that spousal chastisement could not include beatings, but only scolding and "grounding" (the way we might ground a teenager today). But by the time word reached the streets it had become somewhat more expansive: the husband could thrash his wife, but never "with a stick thicker than his thumb."

The fact that we very often pay only lip service today to sexual equality, or honor it in superficial ways, is simply more evidence that "patriarchy" is thoroughly systemic; history can be resisted, but not denied. In any event, from popular master-servant views of matrimony, it was not much of a leap to the common belief, sometimes tacit, other times explicit, that married women themselves could be the subjects of a contract, or even consideration for such bargains — chattels, or, in the modern description, "objects."

In an infamous case from 1302, Sir William Paynel produced a contract for the purchase of his "wife" in an attempt to claim the dower due her — the one-third share of property that became payable to her on her original or "true" husband's death. ("Community property" of roughly 50 per cent per spouse is an idea whose time has only very recently come.) Sir William had bought Margaret Commoys from her husband, John, some time before. The bill of sale read:

> To all the faithful and Christ &c., John Commoys sendeth greeting: Know that I have delivered and committed of my free-will to the Lord William Paynel, Knt., Margaret of Commoys my wife, and have also given and granted, and to the said William released and quit-claimed, all the goods and chattels which the said Margaret has, or hereafter, may have: and also whatever belongs to me of the goods and chattels of the said Margaret with their appurtenances, so that neither I, or any other person in my name, can or ought to exact or claim the goods or chattels of the said Margaret with their appurtenances forever: I will and grant, and by these presents confirm, that the said Margaret shall be and remain with the said Lord William, according to the will of the said William.

In language and effect, the document was a deed. Sir William and Margaret seem also to have presented the king's court with certificates from the Archbishop of Canterbury and the Bishop of Chichester attesting that they had defeated charges of adultery in ecclesiastical court by calling compurgators, witnesses that vouched for the truth of the couple's claim that they lived innocently as man and wife. His Majesty's judges nonetheless found the two to be adulterers, and declared that "William and Margaret do take nothing by their petition but be in mercy [danger of criminal prosecution] for their false claims."

In 1768, the "consideration" in another such transaction, a woman named Ann Parsons, produced the contract for the sale of her own person, asking the court to enjoin her husband, John, from harassing her and her "buyer." "For the support of his extravagancy," she petitioned, John Parsons, clothmaker, had sold her "with all right, property, claim, services, and demands whatsoever" to John Tooker, gentleman. The contract price was six pounds six shillings, about fifteen dollars reckoned at today's exchange rate. The modest price and the rise in social stature were apparently not the only considerations in Ann's transfer of loyalty. Within three months of the sale, John Parsons had turned up at John Tooker's door, demanding more money and threatening Tooker and Ann with death.

Thus, as Thomas Hardy takes some pains to point out, there was long, sad legal precedent for the fateful wife auction in the opening pages of *The Mayor of Casterbridge*, when Michael Henchard, drunk on spiked mead and in a reckless fit of youthful macho, sells his wife, Susan, at a country fair for five guineas (about twelve dollars). Hardy based the sale on two reports he had found in the *Dorset County Chronicle*, Casterbridge being his pseudonym for the English town of Dorchester:

25 May 1826: SALE OF WIFE: Man in Brighton led a tidy-looking woman up to one of the stalls in the market, with a halter round her neck, and offered her for sale. The woman has two children by her husband — one of whom he consents to keep. The other he throws in as a makeweight to the bargain.

6 December 1827: At Buckland near Frome, a labouring man named Charles Pearce sold his wife to shoemaker Elton for £5 and delivered her in a halter in the public street. She seemed very willing. Bells rang.

Thus Hardy makes Susan complicit in the sale, which she believes at the time to be legal. She sees she has no real choice, and she needs somehow to maintain some dignity. Why stand by a husband who seems to value her so little? She has suffered all she can endure moments before the sale is completed, when Henchard asks hotly, "Will anybody buy her?" "I wish somebody would," she replies. "Her present owner is not at all to her liking!"

A wife could be sold for as little as a pint of local ale. Stranger still, the "delivery up" of the woman in a halter was conventional, the parties evidently believing that this lent some formal validity to the transaction, the way, in mediaeval times, a conveyance of land was sealed by the exchange of a clod or twig from that land. The legal propriety of wife selling was established folk wisdom: husbands frequently made such sales at market stalls, in the same way they sold cows and pigs, and even paid tax on them to government regulators. By the time Hardy wrote of the practice, it had become almost banal. A "shipping news" item in the edition of the *Times* for March 30, 1796 reads,

> On Saturday evening last, John Lees, steel-burner, sold his wife for the small sum of sixpence to Samuel Hall, fellmonger [a seller of hides], both of Sheffield. Lees gave Hall one guinea immediately to have her taken off to Manchester the day following by the coach. She was delivered up with an halter round her neck, and the clerk of the market received fourpence for toll. It would be well if some law was inforced to put a stop to such degrading traffic!!

A year later, the traffic was evidently unimpeded:

> On Friday a butcher exposed his wife to sale in Smithfield market, near the Ram Inn, with a halter about her neck and one about her waist, which tied her to a railing, when a hog-driver was the happy purchaser, who gave the husband three guineas and a crown for his departed rib. Pity it is there is no stop to such depraved conduct in the lower order of people.

There is no record of the *Times* ever calling the same sort of flesh-trading among high society "depraved conduct." "Royal weddings" is the usual term, the going price being somewhat higher.

Not altogether surprisingly, the Wild West yields its own example of such a transaction, or a proposed one, although it seems a deed of gift (a "naked promise" insofar as one party gets something for nothing) rather than an offer to sell. It includes the word "bargain," but perhaps only in a reckless sense, on the cruel premise that there would be no takers for such a deal. The document, which a British law journal recently called "A Precedent from America," was originally published in June 1861 in Colorado, having been witnessed by the Clerk of the District Court there.

> Know all men (and women) by these presents that I, John Howard of Canon City of the first part, do hereby give, grant, bargain, convey, and quit claim all my right, title, and interest in and to

the following (un)real estate, to wit: The undivided ancient estate known as Mary Howard, the title of which I acquired by discovery, occupation, possession, and use, situate at present in the town of Denver, Jefferson Territory, together with all the improvements, made and erected by me thereon, with all rents, profits, easements, enjoyments, long suffering, and appurtenances thereto in any wise appertaining, unto — —, of the second part; to have and to hold unto the — —, so long as he can keep her without recourse upon the grantee as endorser.

The offer was probably drawn in the spirit of Mark Twain rather than earnest. The grantor, John Howard, who seems to be misnamed as "grantee" in the deed, had reason to know that it was not legally binding. He was a judge.

Promises to marry have long been enforceable at law one way or another. In 1979, North American newspapers carried a photograph depicting the not unhappy example of a young American named Tim Kowalke, grinning broadly, surrounded by grocery bags and holding in his hands a stack of chocolate-chip cookies. The stack had been culled, evidently, from among the 4,380 such comestibles his former fiancée had agreed to bake for him as settlement for her breach of her promise of matrimony.

But hard questions may arise if someone who promises to wed is already firmly spoken for. Generally, the promisor is held responsible for the pledge, or at least for *breach of warranty* that he was in a position to marry. In England in the 1950s, a man's estate was held additionally liable for his breach of the actual promise to marry after his first wife died and he did not go through a truly legal marriage with his second "wife": though their original "wedding" was invalid (because bigamous), his legitimate wife's death accorded him the capacity to marry anew. Older U.S. law said the same about seductions under promise to marry. In both instances, judges found that, in trusting bigamous cads to be acting in good faith, the women-promisees had undergone a detriment that amounted to sufficient consideration: they had given up something the law recognized as compensable. (The cads were held to their promises at least to the extent of paying money damages.) In this way the judges circumvented the rule that "impossible consideration [marriage by an already-married person] is no consideration."

This is a corollary of the more common rule that "past consideration is no consideration," as where a mistress sues a lover who leaves her in the lurch. To succeed on such a claim, she must have given or given up something other than sexual favors. When in the 1940s a woman threw over the famous actor Wallace Beery for another man, Beery felt his legal obligations to her were mostly past, even though she had given birth to his child. She was, after all, soon to marry the other man. In return for a promise not to sue Beery for paternity and a promise to name the baby "Wallace" or "Wally," the star of *Treasure Island, Grand Hotel* and *The Mighty McGurk* agreed to support and educate the child as if they were all living *en famille*. He would pay the child $25,000 when he turned twenty-one, "to give him a fair start" in adulthood, take out life-insurance policies to secure these payments, and pay the woman anything else necessary to raise the child in a way befitting the son "of a prominent public man of wealth." For each of nine weeks after his son's birth, Beery paid the woman $25. He then repudiated all the woman's claims against him.

At the California District Court of Appeals, Judge Minor Moore could not see how the woman's promises — to name the baby Wallace but not to bring a paternity suit — amounted to sufficient consideration. Beery would have been obliged to support his son (at least to a subsistence level), paternity suit or not. And even if Beery were willing to pay $134,000 to have the baby named after him, people named Wallace were "as numerous as the leaves of Valambrosa." There was no benefit to him, and no detriment to his former lover.

On further appeal, Justice Jesse Carter held that it was "commonly considered a privilege and honor" for a child to bear his father's name. Because of Beery's wealth and fame, "the use of his name and forbearance to bring an action may have great intrinsic value." Any threat by the ex-lover to launch a paternity suit was not duress (which would void the contract), but merely a statement that she would exercise a legal right if Beery didn't agree to her terms. The contract was good: Beery must pay what he had promised.

A few years later, a Maryland court held that a good-faith promise by a new mother not to bring "bastardy proceedings" was sufficient consideration for a man's promise to support the child, even though blood tests later proved the child was not his!

Thus, the collapse of conjugal relationships brings this chapter full circle, logically, and in the sense that separation raises novel consideration problems. In an 1892 separation agreement case, the Supreme Court of Victoria in Australia was asked to solve a problem much like the one that arose around the same time in America, when William Story claimed that refraining from sowing his wild oats was sufficient consideration for his uncle's promise of $5000.

Before 1862, under Anglo-American law, separation agreements were not habitually enforced. The reason was "public policy" again, in its old historical aspect, the legacy, now purely habit and sanctimony, of ecclesiastical law: if husband and wife were one flesh, they couldn't make enforceable contracts with each other, any more than you can sue yourself for breaking a New Year's resolution. Agreements within families, like promises to oneself, were entirely private matters.

But thirty years later, by the time of this Australian case, separation agreements were being treated much like commercial ones. In this instance, the husband had promised to pay six pounds per month to his wife and their five young children, provided the wife (like William Story) "conducted herself with sobriety, and in a respectable, orderly, and virtuous manner," thereby protecting the husband from "personal hate, contempt, and ridicule." When the wife averred that the husband hadn't held up his end of the bargain, Justice John Henry Hood felt her argument was no stronger than the one in the *White v. Bluett* "complaining" case. His lordship could find no evidence that she, herself, had done anything, or refrained from doing anything, she wouldn't have done in any case. A promise to act soberly, respectably and virtuously was "about as vague a promise as can well be imagined." "Acting with sobriety," for instance, could mean that she would be an adamant teetotaler, or that she would drink only until she felt slightly tiddly, or that she might get rip-roaring sozzled, but not in public. And as far as "conducting herself in a virtuous manner," was that "in public or private, and does it include anything short of unchastity?"

But a majority of two judges felt that sufficient consideration flowed both ways. The husband had an assurance that his wife would prove an exemplary mother for his children, and the wife had refrained from exercising her natural rights to let her hair down.

One justice specifically distinguished *White* on the basis that the son there had no *right* to nag his father. But his lordship left it to the philosophers to explain why complaining is a privilege where gallivanting is a right.

CHAPTER THREE

Eaters and Drinkers

"The purchaser cannot be supposed to buy goods to lay them on a dunghill."

In a hurry-up era of disposable everything, this sentiment may no longer ring absolutely true, nor stir the blood the way it must have in 1815, when Lord Chief Justice Ellenborough declaimed it from the bench. Even where we don't buy something to use it once and then dispatch it, consumer protection remains incidental to the profit margin. The huge and noisy war against cancer notwithstanding, merchants sell tobacco to our children as they did in the days of Humphrey Bogart. And despite the "keep-fit" rage, who among us really has the faintest idea where our food has been, under what circumstances? In business, the profit motive is the only motive.

For that reason, Lord Ellenborough's insistence that consumer goods be "merchantable," or reasonably fit to meet the purpose we buy them for, has been codified all across the United States, Britain, and the Commonwealth. But England was well into the Industrial Revolution when his lordship made his dunghill speech. It was the first time in more than five hundred years that complaint was voiced by someone who could make it stick.

Nourishment, biology says, is the prime necessity of life — "metabolism, digestion, catabolism," and only *then* the dunghill — and so it stands to reason that the earliest statutory forms of consumer protection under our legal system were the mediaeval assizes of bread. These served purely to keep the king's peace, at the relatively low cost of full bellies among His Highness's taxpayers, knights and soldiers. First promulgated in 1256, the assizes of bread were designed to discourage sharp practices among bakers — or rather, to protect consumers from the likes of London baker John Brid who in 1327 brought bald-faced highway robbery indoors by stealing his own customers' bread right before their eyes, from homemade dough they had brought to his shop for baking. (Until stone and brick became common in house construction, many residences were built without ovens. Some municipalities provided community ovens, financed by tax revenues, but housewives in other towns had no option but to hire out their baking.) While Brid distracted the customer with chat, an assistant sat under a trapdoor in the shop table and "piecemeal and bit by bit craftily withdrew some of the dough aforesaid." Frustrated in her attempts to practice thrifty homemaking, the customer got less than she paid for in the baking, and Brid allegedly made his own loaves for sale from the sly takings. Less bold knaves sold underweight loaves baked from their own dough.

Breweries were similarly regulated under the assizes of beer. Inspectors, or "conners," would bring charges in feudal or market courts against manufacturers whose ale fell short of the statutory requirements of "clarity and wholesomeness," which the conners assessed by looking at and tasting the ale, and by pouring it on a bench and sitting in it. They wore special leather pants for this purpose; when they rose from the puddle some minutes later, the ale would be judged unwholesome if the conner's trousers stuck to the bench — properly fermented ale not, by these standards, being so sweet as to be sticky. By late in the day, conners sometimes found themselves in gaol for drunk and disorderly conduct, an occupational hazard of the taste test. When Samuel Johnson published his dictionary in 1755, the office of "aleconner" had become "only sinecures for decayed citizens," yet as late as 1905, the Oxford English Dictionary was pointing out that titular "aleconnerships" still existed in Britain.

In earlier times, when personal survival depended on neighborly trust and community vitality, there was nothing quaint about food regulation. Merchants who sold "insufficient" loaves or impure beer, hid rotten meat and fish amid the fresh or mixed "into a sacke of wheat a pottle of sande of the sea" could end up local pariahs.

Mediaeval town records in England chronicle a long procession of shady and negligent tradesmen sentenced to the pillory or trundled through villages on the ducking stool or "Castigator," a chair set on a beam that was mounted on a fulcrum. Offenders — tradesmen and other community nuisances such as "common scolds" — were dipped into the nearest pond or river. To dramatize the offender's outcast state, the Castigator's chair was sometimes a "close-stool," a version of the modern toilet — a chamber pot enclosed in a box or stool. So serviceable was the close-stool as an instrument of public humiliation that it might even explain why the punishment was called "ducking": a credible theory has it that "ducking-stool" may derive not from "duck," but "cuck," Anglo-Saxon for "to pass excrement." The Castigator's older name, "cucking-stool," reinforces this toilet theme, as might the fact that urinals were sometimes suspended from the necks of assize-offenders, who were then driven through town on jackasses. Whetstones could also be hung on them during the ride, perhaps as a totem of their sharp and wounding ways. Some convicted bakers rode the tumbrel (from the French "*tombereau*," "dung cart") wearing a necklace of their impugned loaves.

Still, during the next half-millenium, burgeoning mercantilism came to favor the seller. As the marketplace expanded, community ties, the sort that develop in towns so small "everybody knows your business," were stretched and weakened. As settlements grew into large cities with dense populations, bargainers were often strangers and their transactions were hard to police. To maintain at least an appearance of control, the courts began to enunciate a doctrine that has become a cornerstone of contract law, demanding sophistication of the everyday shopper: except in extreme cases, the law would not interfere in a bargain.

At first, nobody said as much out loud. But early on, even as the Bible was being translated into Jacobean English, so that redemption would be available to all, the courts were taking this more worldly view. Two extraordinary examples crop up at the bottom of the food chain.

A deal made at the turn of the seventeenth century stipulated that Morgan could have James's horse if Morgan gave James one barleycorn for each nail in the horse's shoes, "doubling it every nail" — one barleycorn for the first nail, two for the second, four for the third, eight for the fourth, and so on, through thirty-two nails — eight per shoe. Poor old Morgan did not twig to what he was getting into until someone explained that "doubling it every nail" amounted to four thousand bushels of barley — 4,294,967,295 barleycorns. Despite the enormity of the debt, and the obvious fact that there could have been no real "meeting of the minds" between buyer and seller, Justice Hyde at the Hereford Assizes declared the contract valid, only to compromise it himself moments later, directing the jury to give James not the four thousand bushels but the value of the horse, "being eight pounds."

In a similar but even more awesome case, for five pounds Whitacre had agreed to deliver to Thornburgh "two grains of rye corn on Monday the 29th of March, and four grains of rye corn on Monday the next following, and eight grains of rye corn on Monday next after the Monday last mentioned . . . etc. *et progressa sic deliberaret quolibet alio di Lunae successive infra unun annum ad eodem 29 Martii bis tot grana secalis quot die Lunae proximo praecedente respective deliberanda forent, etc.*" (and so on, exponentially, every Monday for a year).

Before the case was left to the jury, William Salkeld, acting for the defendant Whitacre, moved to have it dismissed. As his client could not possibly supply this quantity of grain, the deal, he argued, was completely invalid. "All the rye in the world was not so much," he said, and cited three sorts of contractual impossibility: agreements founded in immorality, natural impossibilities and human impossibilities, "as to touch the heavens or go to Rome in a day." His client's difficulty, as Salkeld saw it, fell into the last category. He compared the bargain to a tenancy in which the tenant agrees that at his death a rose will be paid to the lord of his land. In such a case, the lord could not take action for payment against the tenant's estate until roses were in season.

When the court pointed out that *James v. Morgan* had proclaimed a similar seemingly impossible contract binding, Salkeld attempted to sidestep that precedent. Payment of the four billion barleycorns owed to farmer Morgan "was possible to be performed," he argued (lacking the skepticism of a farmer), "though it was an ill bargain." But by any accounting the 1,123,903,923,659,840 grains of rye owed by Whitacre are more than staggering.

Chief Justice Holt seems to have replied, pedantically, that "*quolibet alio die Lunae*" meant every *other* Monday, "and that could bring the contract nearer to the defendant's ability of performance." A helpful note in *Lord Raymond's Reports* makes the resulting amount "125 quarters, fifty two, 524,288,000" (more than a thousand bushels). All reports are silent on whether the judge really made these calculations before he refused to dismiss the claim, confidently proclaiming in the spirit of *James v. Morgan* that "though it seems to be a great quantity, yet the jury will consider the folly of the defendant, and give reasonable damages."

Lord Raymond describes what happened next: "Perceiving the opinion of the court to be against his client, Salkeld offered plaintiff Thornburgh "his half crown and his cost, which was accepted of, and so no judgment was given in the case." Evidently hesitant to publicize a Pyrrhic victory, Salkeld does not mention the offer of settlement in his own report series.

In theory, at least, Morgan and Whitacre were made liable for their breathtaking carelessness — or ignorance — while the judges, presaging their later rule that the law will not make new deals for aggrieved bargainers, technically condoned the sharp practice of plaintiffs James and Thornburgh. While agreeing with Salkeld in principle that contracts to do the impossible cannot be enforced, the courts have often enforced them anyway, even in modern times.

In 1729, a court held a tenancy contract valid even though the judges required payment of a third of a penny, and it allowed the landlord to take the defendant's heifer in default. The court cited as precedent the venerable *Marsham v. Buller*, 1618, in which a jury assessed damages of half a farthing. Buller's lawyer had argued that the judgment could not be executed because there was no such coin, only to be lectured by the judge, Sir John Dodridge, that, "Although your purse be full, in Oxford you can buy a beer for half a farthing, and Haughton [a sheriff?] can execute judgment against you of half a farthing for an egg." Perhaps his lordship meant that you could be charged half a farthing for a beer on the theory that this was the price per half-pint, and that you would eventually order the other half; similarly, one egg could be worth half a farthing in the sense that eventually you would owe the seller for more, in common currency. A dozen, by such a reckoning, would come to six farthings.

Of course, these are the rare cases, their eccentricity being the very reason they are remembered by legal history. The courts have resorted to such metaphysics in contract law, otherwise the most brass-tacks conservative of all legal categories, only when there has been no other way of throwing their weight behind the laissez-faire bulwarks of capitalist society — the central assumption being that the marketplace should regulate itself. In this respect, *James* and *Whitacre* are basically legal assertions of social Darwinism — survival of the fittest in an unregulated market "jungle."

Indeed, one "jungle" theory of biology holds that the human body is so poorly adapted for survival in nature because once *homo sapiens* extended its physical prowess through the use of tools, evolution became concentrated in the brain. Why carry around long, heavy arms and fists when your brain can design ever more sophisticated sticks to do what your appendages would do, but many times better than they could do it, and only as needed? The body was thus left completely dependent on cognition to arrange its sustenance, protection, and comfort.

Contract law has followed a similar course, periodically fitting an improvised tool to a stiff and aging body, rather like an old man who gives in and buys an ear trumpet instead of a hearing aid. It makes a virtue of selfishness, its basic interest being the protection of the status quo — pursuing that profit motive, undisturbed by regulation — which it confuses with preservation of the species. Century upon century it insists, "Every bargainer for himself."

Insular and self-absorbed, it will not change unless irritated beyond complacency. And even then, it is likely to stretch a point rather than change one, or cannibalize other areas of the law rather than adapt with innovations of its own.

When business law is loathe to disturb contracts that don't give buyers the food or drink they bargain for, the criminal law will often be obliged to do it instead. Some commentators call the correspondence between major branches of the law "cross-pollinization"; but it could as easily be said that contract law is parasitic. The impossibility problems in *James* and *Whitacre* are analogous to those in criminal law, where it is now settled that just as you can be held to an impossible bargain, you can be convicted of attempting to pick an empty pocket, rob an empty store, or perhaps even kill a dead person. The crime consists in the attempt itself, the desire and endeavor to rob or kill. Other commercial cases pass the buck from private civil law straight into the law of offenses against state and community, casting a backward glance at the quasi-criminal type of regulation established under the assizes of bread and beer. In pushing only select commercial behavior outside its pale in this way, and redefining it as an "offense against the body politic," business preserves the myth that it successfully regulates itself in the public interest, and that government should keep its hands off.

There is American authority, for example, that, as a party to a practical joke, a druggist who sells candy adulterated with a laxative can be prosecuted for criminal battery. Only very recently has such behavior become an "unfair trade practice" within commercial law proper. Again, the full weight of state sanction has been brought to bear where coffee is cut with beets and acorns, and "pure" cocoa "extended" with brick dust.

Although Britain's Conservative government recently made Sunday shopping legal, for centuries "Lord's day" legislation forbade it. Violations were criminal offenses (and remain so in parts of Canada and other jurisdictions); Sunday shopping was not bargaining for profit, it was something *immoral*, bargaining *on Sunday*, violating the *social* contract. State sanction again claimed divine inspiration. In terms of transactions concerning food, from 1677 the *Sunday Observance Act* had allowed only "dressing of meat in families, or dressing or selling of meat in inns, cook's shops, or victualling houses" — on the breathtaking presumption, evidently, that God (through His delegates in the government) would exempt the better class of food retailer from the Sabbath requirements, but no one else. In the absence of any law or principle that accorded equal rights to all shoppers whether their tastes and budgets ran to rump roasts each weekend or only to sardines, British judges were at pains to dodge the ethnocentricism of the *Sunday Observance Act* by declaring that fish, not to mention French fries, could be meat.

The Law Journal is poignant about the evidence in the case of Mr. Bullen, a Blackburn "chipped potato dealer" — a fish-and-chips restaurateur — prosecuted under the *Sunday Observance Act* in 1905:

> It was proved that the appellant in the course of his business, cut up and cooked or fried potatoes, sometimes alone and sometimes with fish, and that these articles had become a popular food with the working classes. The fried potatoes and fish, together or separately, were served on the appellant's premises as well as off, and were always sold warm. The customers, when supplied off the premises, often brought their own receptacles for the food, but were sometimes supplied in paper bags belonging to the appellant. On Sunday, January 22, 1905, the appellant was carrying on his usual business, there being customers upon his premises eating the chipped potatoes, others who purchased articles of food and took them away in bags or basins, and some who ate the food in the street near the appellant's shop.

Mr. Bullen was convicted. While the landed gentry were free to shop for their Sunday joint, those of more modest tea-time habits were accessories to a crime. Bullen's modest "chippy" was not to be confused in the law courts ("open to all, just like the Ritz Hotel") with a legitimate "victualling house."

Happily, Mr. Bullen could afford to seek a second opinion. On his appeal to the Court of King's Bench Lord Alverstone, the chief justice, found that, come Sunday it "would be ridiculous to say that, although a man may cook mutton, he must not cook an eel pie." Even if some customers bought only French fries for their dinner, at common law French fries were meat. As for fish, well, one bloke's meat, after all, is another man's *poisson*. . . .

But not his *crème glacé*. In 1915, a man named Slater attempted to stretch the analogy to ice cream. On Boxing Day (December 26, the day in Britain and Canada traditionally set aside for packaging gifts for the poor), which also happened to be a Sunday, Slater bought an ice-cream sandwich from Berni, "a licensed refreshment house keeper," only to have his pleasure in consuming it interrupted by a constable who charged him with "aiding and abetting" Berni in violating the *Sunday Observance Act*. He was under arrest, for eating ice cream.

At trial, Slater argued that ice cream was a "sweetmeat," and therefore a form of meat within the *Sunday Observance Act* exemptions. But the justices decided that the definition of "ice cream" was irrelevant and convicted him.

On appeal, Slater's lawyer re-emphasized the meat argument: the constituent elements of the ice cream, he said, milk, sugar, eggs, and egg powder (sandwiched between two biscuits), could each be described as "meat" under certain usages of that word in English. Indeed, the Oxford English Dictionary suggests this view, repeating Samuel Johnson's definition of meat as "food in general; anything used as nourishment for men or animals; usually, solid food, in contradistinction to drink. (The OED adds that this usage had become "archaic and dialectical.") It also makes special mention of "green meat," "grass or green vegetables used for food or fodder."

Justice Charles Darling allowed that meat could be "anything that can be eaten," as in such expressions as "the meat of an egg," "meat and drink," and "one man's meat is another man's poison." But he held anyway that meat could not be ice cream. "Meat" in the *Sunday Observance Act* had nothing to do with proverbial usage. (Legally, this is debatable: where a word is not defined in a statute, generally it must be given its "ordinary" meaning.)

Justice Thomas Horridge tersely agreed. "There is nothing in the term 'ice-cream,'" he said, "as there is in the term 'mutton chop,' which would make it necessary for us to say that ice cream fell within the exemptions."

But given recent developments in both England and North America, Justice Darling has had the last word. He concluded his opinion in *Slater* with: "I think it is plain that many judges, not liking this kind of legislation — I do not like it myself — have tried to get out of the statute by holding or suggesting that all kinds of things might be 'meat' although they were not. In my opinion, the best way to attain that object is to construe it strictly, in the way the Puritans who procured it would have construed it; if that is done it will very soon be repealed."

Whether we get what we bargain for may depend on how we describe it. If we decide to call our economy car "Nova" (from the Latin for "new", "modern", "fresh," "young"), we may find, as Chevrolet did in the 1970s, that South Americans will refuse to buy it because in Spanish *"no va"* means "won't go." In Germany, the corporate slogan "Come alive! Drink Pepsi!" was translated as "Come out of the grave with Pepsi!" Some Anglicisms that would kill a product in an English-speaking country can assure its success in Japan, where a non-dairy "cream product" is called *"Creap,"* chocolate in a box designed to resemble the box Band-Aids come in is labeled *"Hand-Maid Queer Aids"* and a chocolate bar is sold under the moniker *"Carap"* — only slightly less appetizing than *"Crunky Bar."*

If you do attempt to market a rose by another name, it had better be at least as original as these. Otherwise, if you haven't offended the common law, you will have offended the regal principles of chancery.

In its early days, the common law proclaimed itself Heaven's lieutenant, vigilant on the front of human frailty, steeling itself against pleas that we all have momentary lapses or can't always rein in our youthful, hyperactive hormones. As a world-view imposed by human beings *upon* human beings, this was doomed to failure. Its rigidity proved crippling as early as the twelfth century, when citizens who could get no relief at common law began to take their problems directly to the lord chancellor, the personal agent of the sovereign. Although nominally bound by the substantive common law, the lord chancellor was free from the strictures of court procedure; he could decide disputes "on the equities," a practice that became so popular an entire court system of equity was soon established in chancery and began competing for business with the common-law courts. Equity has since been woven into the common law, the most familiar of its contributions being injunctions and the allowance of specific performance in contracts (discussed in Chapter Seven). But originally, it was an alternative to the common law, its competitor as well as its bulwark, keeping aggrieved plaintiffs from taking the law into their own hands.

While the common law said that an action could not arise out of a person's own unlawful conduct, equity could afford a somewhat higher threshold of sympathy. Its own maxim about duplicitous litigants went, "You must come to equity with clean hands." The common law refused legal assistance even if you had "dirtied your hands" inadvertently, through negligence or through some minor indiscretion. But equity made allowances for human foible. It has scowled only at deliberate acts of malfeasance, such as fraud, adapting handily to the otherwise laissez-faire preferences of the commercial world.

In 1920, such equitable sootiness was alleged on both sides of a dispute between Coca-Cola, on the one hand, and the associated Southern Koke Company and Koke Companies of America and Arkansas, on the other. Coca-Cola had brought a trademark action, alleging that Koke was "passing off" its product, a caramel-colored soda manufactured and packaged in the Coca-Cola mode, as the wildly popular Real Thing. Coke sought an injunction against the manufacture of Koke's soda pop and an accounting of profits — payment to them of all money made by Koke using the Koke name, as well as the money made under the other name the defendants used to market their clone product, "Dope."

Within a few years of its debut on the market, Coca-Cola had become widely known as "Coke" and "Dope" (homage to the fact that early recipes called for cocaine as well as caffeine). On this evidence, Coke won its injunction in the Arizona District Court. But the Koke companies appealed, alleging that Coca-Cola's business practices disentitled them to "injunctive relief."

As "equitable remedies," injunctions are available only to those who seek them "with clean hands." The Arizona Circuit Court agreed with Koke that Coca-Cola's hands were soiled. "For many years," Judge Erskine Ross found,

> the coca of which its [Coke's] compound was in large part made, contained the deadly drug cocaine, and the caffeine which constituted the other main ingredient, was derived mainly, and indeed almost exclusively, not from cola nuts, but from tea leaves. Yet the labels with which the preparation was adorned contained pictures of coca leaves and cola nuts, and [the drink] was widely advertised and sold, first under the name of "Coca-Cola Syrup and Extract," next as "Coca-Cola Syrup," and finally as "Coca-Cola," as "a valuable brain tonic," and an "ideal nerve tonic and

stimulant," as a cure of "headache, neuralgia, hysteria, and melancholy, and of nervous afflictions," under which reputation a tremendous consumption was built up.

By the time of the legal action, the cocaine in Coca-Cola had in fact been eliminated, while the caffeine was still derived mostly from sources other than cola. Finding that the "tremendous consumption" was based on misrepresentation, the court held that Coke's own business practices had been "deceptive, false, fraudulent, and unconscionable," disentitling them to equitable relief.

Coke had suffered such frontal attack before. Its steady success during the 1890s and into the new century had made it a target for knock-off artists, and the world's most famous cola company was becoming expert at litigation. In 1912, for example, it had sued the Gay-Ola company, which claimed to have discovered Coke's formula and was selling an imitation at a discounted price. In its promotional material, Gay-Ola offered to ship its knock-off to bottlers and restaurateurs in plain wrap, if necessary, although they had gone out of their way to imitate Coca-Cola's distinctive red and its "script" typography. Gay-Ola's sales material included a testimonial from a soda jerk: "No one can tell it from Coca-Cola, and I sell it for Coca-Cola, and everyone says I have the best Coca-Cola in the city."

During hearings, Gay-Ola, like Koke after them, counter-claimed that Coca-Cola itself was in the business of deceiving consumers, but led no evidence on this "clean-hands" issue. On November 7, 1912, Judge Arthur Denison, of the Circuit Court of Appeals for the Sixth District, concluded that the "underlying intent" of Gay-Ola's business practices was "to perpetrate a fraud" on the public, and to compete unfairly with Coca-Cola. He issued an injunction in favor of Coke and ordered Gay-Ola to pay Coke's costs.

Not so lucky on its first appeal against the Koke companies, Coca-Cola now soldiered on to the Circuit Court of Appeals, and there found a sympathetic ear in Justice Oliver Wendell Holmes. After processing, the only thing left of the coca leaves in Coca-Cola was "a little tannic acid and still less chlorophyll," Holmes ruled. And it was true that the cola nut "furnishes but a very small portion of the caffeine." But at issue was "a popular drink," not a drug (even though some of the goodwill originally associated with Coke was related to its narcotic element). Coca-Cola was no longer representing its soda as some magical medicine or aqua vitae, but it had nevertheless become so popular that "it hardly would be too much to say that the drink characterizes the name as much as the name the drink." Unlike Koke, Coca-Cola was not attempting to put something over on the public.

But all was not lost for the sundry Koke companies. While in some restaurants you could ask for a Dope and minutes later be served a Coke, "dope" — a "featureless word known even to the language of those who are incapable of discriminating speech" — "would equally have been used to call for anything else having about it a faint aureole of poison." It was common currency, not a Coca-Cola trademark; for that matter, the company did not like to have their product associated with the word. If Koke wanted to use it as a product name, good luck to them.

While "Coke" has become synonymous with "cola," the Coca-Cola bottlers do not claim trademark in the latter word. Indeed, when a commercial name exceeds mere popularity to become common currency, or a "generic" label, brand managers can break out in cold sweats.

The Xerox Corporation has expended huge sums to remind the world that a photocopy is a photocopy, but only a Xerox machine can xerox. A paper tissue in many homes may be a Kleenex even if it's a Scotties, while the household children, roustabouts today but the shoppers of tomorrow, don't make the distinction between Jell-O and gelatin that merchandisers do. When corporate panic over such confusion becomes really endemic, the brand managers go to court, where brows are painfully furrowed, language teased and strained in proceedings that suggest Kafka as interpreted by the Marx brothers.

The difficulty is that the typical corporation wants to have its Jell-O and eat it, too; it puts its all into making its product shine as distinctive, but at the same time otherwise detests eccentricity. Catholic tastes and individual predilection destroy the economy of the company's marketing schemes, which depend absolutely on every consumer harboring identical needs, desires and motivations. Where such homogeneity does not exist, the company will do everything it can to create it through public relations. A predictable market is a captive one. "Economies of scale" crumble when you must tool up differently to cater to individual penchants.

If business craves homogeneity and worships monomania (how else explain why a man devotes the best years of his life to increasing the annual sales of dish-washing soap or disposable diapers?), it could be that in 1906, the Bile Bean Manufacturing Corporation of Leeds was acting in perfectly good faith when its officers insisted that each time the public thought of "bile beans," it had in mind nothing but their specific product.

The defender in the suit, an Edinburgh druggist named Davidson, admitted to Lord Ardwall, the Scottish Lord Ordinary, that, in marketing a product identical to BBM's Bile Beans for Biliousness, he was attempting to capitalize on their huge advertising expenditures and consequent success. But the courts found that it was the complainer who had the dirtiest hands.

What really exercised the judges, at trial as well as on appeal, was that, as Lord Ardwall put it, BBM's product was based "entirely upon fraud, impudence, and advertisement, although it may be that the pill is as effective as any ordinary pill so compounded."

The company's founder was Charles Fulford, a Canadian who had worked for five years as an assistant in a drug store but was otherwise untrained in chemistry or pharmacology. During his employment as a druggist, he was struck with the success of a product called "Pink Pills for Pink People." Attracted by the alliteration, his first solo venture entailed marketing his own "Gould's Tiny Tonic Pills."

These had fairly tiny success, but Fulford persisted. Although in court he claimed invention of bile beans, *per se*, the evidence suggested that during his drugstore work he may have encountered a product called Smith's Bile Beans. These were sold exclusively in the United States, where "bean" had for some time been used to describe any ovular pill. Some of these pills were styled as patent medicine: "Bright's Kidney Beans," "Candy Regulating Beans," "Lyon Drug Company's Female Beans," "Nerve Beans," and the Smith product. Fulford anyway bought Smith's British rights and set about marketing his own bile beans for biliousness across the world, carefully avoiding the United States and Canada, which Smith had locked up.

Central to Fulford's promotion was an explorer called Charles Forde, invented by Fulford and modeled on himself, albeit very loosely. Forde was "an eminent scientist" whom Australian aboriginals had introduced to "a natural vegetable substance" of great purgative and curative powers, now a constituent of Bile Beans for Biliousness. Fulford published several musical advertisements having to do with Forde, including the "Bile Bean March" (unfortunately, its lyrics are not preserved in the law reports), and distributed flyers, placards and eighty-three million pamphlets recounting Forde's exploits. The print advertising was "often embellished with pictorial representations of the healthy savage and with pictures of the imaginary scientist duly bearded and begoggled, having the precious root pointed out to him by the Australian native." One of the pamphlets began:

> The secret of the natives. More important than the whereabouts of hidden gold was the secret of the ancient natives of Australia. For untold ages they had handed down to them the great secret of how certain native herbs cured the diseases to which they were subject, and thus preserved them in excellent health. . . .
>
> Not only from the writings and observations of Captain Cook but from their own experiments, also, scientists have long been impressed with the superiority of vegetable medicines. Some years back, Charles Forde, an eminent scientist, thoroughly investigated the healing extracts and essences of Australian roots and herbs, and after long research he found himself the discoverer of a natural vegetable substance which had the power of acting in the human system in the same way as nature's own animal substance, bile, and which was beyond all doubt the finest remedy yet discovered for all liver and digestive disorders.

Another pamphlet boasted,

> The best laboratories, the most modern plant, all that science dictated as being best for the purpose, was requisitioned in the compounding of this substance into convenient medicinal form; and the result of it all was the production a few years back of Charles Forde's Bile Beans — the most perfect medicine of modern times.

In fact, Bile Beans for Biliousness were compounded of chemicals in the laboratories of Parke, Davis, and at other pharmaceutical companies in the United States, and were imported from Detroit. Yet Fulford argued that the Charles Forde hokum was "mere puffery," an innocent sales gimmick (in this instance something like today's Tony the Tiger or Keebler elves; when taxpayer Ruffolo sued the Canadian government in 1988 for failing to keep election promises, the judge dismissed the promises as "mere puffery"). At worst, he said, his claim about the origin of the beans was a misrepresentation "collateral" to the name of the product, and did not affect his property rights in the name, *per se*.

But at both trial and appeal, the courts held that the Forde story and the product name were inextricable. The success of Fulford's beans had depended upon it. Even the box, which was very different in design from Davidson's, identified the pills as "Charles Forde's Bile Beans for Biliousness." The fraud went straight to the name, and Fulford could not obtain "assistance from the law for a business based on unblushing falsehood for the purpose of defrauding the public into a totally false belief as to the origin and material" of his product.

Business conservatism concerns itself with matters of the heart only insofar as they "interface" with bellies and bank accounts. Courts involved in commercial litigation, like people in the commercial world generally, prefer to keep business and personal affairs apart, rather like Church and State are supposed to be in modern constitutional democracies. In an environment indifferent, or even hostile, to sentiment and abstraction, matters of emotion, however much they may figure in the mercenary psychology (more than one Napoleonic tycoon has built his fortune on the foundation of insecurity and fear), are likely to seem too private, too "touchy-feely" or soft.

As it is with hearts, so with minds. Since the late 1800s, under the more visceral law of tort (the branch of law that holds us accountable for the harm we do to others, deliberately or negligently), courts have awarded damages for mental suffering and "emotional shock." The famous insanity defense of the criminal courts — that to be culpable, an accused person must have understood the "nature and quality" of his behavior, or understood that it was wrong — was formulated in 1843, when Daniel M'Naghten, a Scottish schizophrenic, was acquitted of an attempt on the life of Prime Minister Robert Peel. As psychology has become more acceptable in society at large, so has it been admitted more readily to the courtroom — too readily, some would say, or too recklessly, in criminal law. But while contracts made by "the mentally disordered" have long been subject to cancellation ("voidable," in the jargon) until very recently, judges felt they could not put a dollar figure on the mental pain caused by problems in the marketplace. Anguish was an intangible, or was not something indulged by business.

Rather than own up to such robotic literalism, however, judges had usually said that they could not assess damages for mental distress because it was "too remote" a consequence of contractual breach. Using the language of precedent, the hoary rule that damages "must flow naturally from the breach" and be "reasonably foreseeable" at the time of agreement, they hardened their hearts, and the arteries of the common law, dreamily contemplating the past.

So *Jarvis v. Swan Tours*, where judicial scrutiny was again concentrated on finger-food — potato chips, this time, and stale nutcakes — was an awakening. Contract law came groggily out of its after-teatime nap to notice at last that the everyday bargainer was flesh and blood, with intangible, but still real and reasonable, needs and feelings.

According to Lord Denning, Master of the Rolls in the English Court of Appeal, Jarvis, a young and marriageable solicitor from Barking, in southeastern England, paid Swans £63.45 in 1969 for a ski-holiday package to Morlialp, Giswil, in central Switzerland. He had been sold on the resort by one of Swans' brochures, which promised a beautiful alpine setting "with a wide variety of fine ski-runs, a skating-rink and an exhilarating toboggan run."

"Why," the brochure asked,

did we choose the Hotel Krone? Mainly and most of all, because of the "GEMUTLICHKEIT" and friendly welcome you will receive from Herr and Frau Weibel. The Hotel Krone has its own Alphütte Bar which will be open several evenings a week. No doubt you will be in for a great time, when you book this houseparty holiday. Mr. Weibel, the charming owner, speaks English.

Mr. Weibel, it turned out, didn't, which made life rather difficult for Jarvis during the second week of his stay, considering that he was the only guest. There had been thirteen skiers the first week, but Jarvis had expected to be one of a "houseparty" of some thirty or so people. Two weeks out of 52, he felt he'd earned a bit of a bust up.

The ski runs were all some distance from the hotel, and, at that, the only skiing available was on "shorties," skis about three feet long. In the second week, discouraged, solitary Jarvis managed to scare up some longer skis "for a couple of days, but then, because of the boots, his feet got rubbed and he could not continue even with the long skis."

A promised "yodler evening" turned out to be "one man from the locality who came in his working clothes for a little while, and sang four or five songs quickly." The Alphütte Bar was situated in "an unoccupied annexe which was only open one evening." And then, of course there were, or weren't, the *Sacher torte* and *streudel*: the brochure had promised afternoon tea and cake for seven days, but "the only cakes for tea were potato crisps and little dry nutcakes."

Jarvis sued his travel agent, claiming misrepresentation and seeking a refund as well as reimbursement of two weeks' salary. At trial, on the logic that he had received about half of what he'd contracted for, he was awarded £31.72. But in the Court of Appeal, his little sixty-four pound case opened new vistas to contract law when the judges allowed him additional recovery for disappointment, distress and frustration. As Lord Justice Herbert Edmund Davies put it, damages in such circumstances could not be "confined to matters of physical inconvenience and discomfort, or even to quantifying the difference between such items as the expected delicious Swiss cakes and the depressingly dessicated biscuits and crisps." The judges refused to give Jarvis the £93.27 he claimed in salary, but awarded him a total of £125 — making for mental distress damages of just a penny more than that salary figure: £125 = £31.72 (damages awarded to Jarvis at trial for Swans' breach of contract) + £93.28. Since then, damages for mental distress have become almost commonplace in some areas of contract law, especially for breach of employment agreements.

Jarvis sits at one of several intersections on the modern road to justice where tort principles have worked profound effects on contract. It is, in a sense, a logical extension of perhaps the grandest instance, *Donoghue v. Stevenson*, a foundational case in what we understand today to be "consumer protection." Both cases use the law of tort, more liberal in outlook than the law of contract, to circumscribe mercantilism, entrenching boundaries around the influence of the Industrial Revolution. Where *Jarvis* extends the reach of "compensable damages," *Donoghue* enlarges the range of defendants a buyer may sue. By permitting consumers to bring actions against manufacturers instead of just retailers, it has made the consumer suit double- (or multiple-) barrelled: if an action fails against one defendant, it might succeed against the other. If one defendant is liable but "impecunious," maybe the other can afford to pay damages.

Pre-existing law had usually dictated that liability could not be assessed so far down the contractual chain. When a decomposed snail shot out with the ginger beer Mrs. Donoghue was pouring from a bottle over her ice cream, her dealings, after all, had been with the café owner, Minchella — not with ginger beer manufacturer Stevenson. Stevenson, the law before this had said, was not a party to the contract for the ice cream soda, and therefore could never be held negligent in causing the young shop assistant shock, nausea and severe gastroenteritis.

But Mrs. Donoghue's lawyer decided to attack Stevenson on the theory that insofar as the ginger-beer bottle was opaque and sealed, Minchella could not have known of the adulteration, nor should he even have suspected it. (And, as a large manufacturer, Stevenson presumably had more resources to draw on to pay plaintiff's damages than a small businessman like Minchella would.) Relying on precedent, and probably horrified by the prospect for manufacturers in all fields of business if Mrs. Donoghue won the day, Stevenson's lawyers did everything they could to get the case dismissed on a preliminary motion, before the case could be tried on its merits. This motion went all the way to the appellate committee of the House of Lords, inspiring one of the most famous dicta in the common law, Lord Atkin's "neighbour" speech:

> The rule that you are to love your neighbour becomes in law, you must not injure your neighbour, and the lawyer's question, Who is my neighbour? receives a restricted reply. You must take

reasonable care to avoid acts or omissions which you can reasonably foresee would be likely to injure your neighbour. Who, then, in law is my neighbour? The answer seems to be — persons who are so closely and directly affected by my act that I ought reasonably to have them in contemplation as being so affected when I am directing my mind to the acts or omissions which are called in question.

Lord Atkin was saying that the trial should go ahead because there was a strong possibility that Stevenson was liable for the snail in the ginger ale. It was at least arguable that consumers — "neighbours" — like young Ms. Donoghue ought to have been in his "contemplation" when he manufactured the drink.

The proposition became the foundation of all modern negligence law, including negligence arising in contractual relationships, such as the purchase of ice-cream sodas. But ironically, this revolutionary action itself never went to trial, after all. Stevenson died before the trial date, prompting Mrs. Donoghue to settle for one hundred pounds.

Thanks to Lord Ellenborough's dunghill dictum of 1815, contract law already had a remedy against retailers of unfit food. In some cases damage was clear and there was no one else to blame. If a visitor to a café died of ptomaine from the tuna, it could be awfully difficult to lay the fault at his own kitchen door. But while generally there were more products at better prices than ever before, in the survival-of-the-fittest jungle of the laissez-faire economy the seemingly banal idea that consumer goods should be reasonably fit to meet their buyers' needs had got off to a shaky start. "Merchantability" was a legal formula of only occasional practical impact.

Caveat emptor had been in the ascendant, after all, from the late middle ages, and it was only against the weight of five hundred years of history, and very much in spite of its own inclinations, that the Industrial Revolution helped to shift the balance back toward the consumer. By the end of the nineteenth century, the commercial world was having almost everything on its own terms, putting so much pressure on the consuming public that something had to give somewhere. Business had become so headstrong that its habits of exploitation showed up in defective products — frequently enough, with sufficiently serious consequences, that, in the courts of justice, the customer was at least occasionally right.

One of the period's most remarkable statements to this effect is, aptly enough, another case about a young girl and allegedly comestible sea-life. It is an Irish case, about crabs.

At around 5:30 on July 24, 1901, Ellen Donovan had gone to the fishmonger's for her grandmother, Mrs. Wallis. When she asked the shop manager for two crabs, he said he had no live specimens, only boiled ones. Ellen replied that she would take "two nice fresh crabs" anyway, for her grandmother's tea. She selected one in particular, but after inspecting and hefting it, the shop manager put it aside and selected two others. Again asking if these were "nice and fresh," Ellen paid sixpence for the crabs and left the shop.

After tea that night, both Ellen and Mrs. Wallis fell ill. Mrs. Wallis "was confined to her room for five weeks, and the medical evidence showed that she suffered from poisoning." A physician evidently testified that both women were near death, or, as Lord Justice Gerald Fitz Gibbon later said, "The seller got the price; the buyer paid it, and was nearly killed."

The fishmonger testified that out of the 36 crabs he'd sold of that same lot, he had traced twenty-six, not counting Ellen's two. None of those had given their consumers any trouble. The shop manager testified that if anything had been wrong with the crabs, he would have detected it by heft and appearance.

The Irish Court of Appeal ultimately awarded Mrs. Wallis one hundred fifty pounds in damages. In doing so, the court relied on the *Sale of Goods Act*, the statute in which Lord Ellenborough's rules on merchantability had been codified. The act, which is still on the books, says that if a buyer makes known to a seller the "particular purpose" the buyer wants the goods for, and in doing so "relies on the seller's skill or judgment," the seller is bound by a special warranty — namely, that the goods will be fit for that particular purpose. Viewers of "The People's Court" will have hard Judge Wapner refer to this requirement, now part of the *Uniform Commercial Code* of the United States, and of the British and Canadian *Sale of Goods Acts*, as "an implied warranty of merchantability."

Although Ellen had been free to inspect the crabs, the court found that she had relied on the fishmonger's judgment that no "latent defects" existed in them — that they were "nice and fresh for tea." Even if the fishmonger had not guaranteed their quality in so many words, at law, he was assumed to have done so. Finally, commercial law was crying "*Caveat venditor!*" — or at least it was finally putting a fence around caveat emptor. That latter maxim, Lord Justice Fitz Gibbon remarked, "does not mean — in the law or Latin — that the buyer must 'take [his] chance'; it means that he must 'take care' " — as Ellen had done, by checking twice that she was buying seafood fit for that evening's meal.

Then again, one account of her testimony suggests she was so well-versed in *Sale of Goods* law that her evidence was, well, fishy.

By this report, Ellen had told the trial court that she "asked the shopman for a nice cooked crab, telling him I wanted it for Mrs. Wallis's supper, so as to make known to him the purpose for which it was to be used."

Sir Peter O'Brien of Kilfenora, the trial judge and chief justice of the Irish Court of King's Bench, could hardly believe what he was hearing. "You said that? In those very words?"

Ellen said she had.

"Remarkable the strides education is taking. Go on."

"Well, then," Ellen continued, "when I had told him that, he looked at the crabs, and he selected one and gave it to me. So I, relying on his skill and judgment, took it."

Lord Chief Justice O'Brien asked her where she had been educated.

"At the Ursuline Convent, Blackrock, my Lord," she replied, prompting his lordship to wonder "since when have the Ursuline sisters included section fourteen of the *Sale of Goods Act* in their curriculum."

Ellen couldn't say.

"What admirable nuns!" Chief Justice O'Brien exclaimed, with, as the reporter of this version of the case notes, sarcasm that was lost on the jury.

What had become clear more lately is that Mrs. Wallis's solicitor was her son, Ellen's uncle.

Consumer protection enjoyed a short-lived heyday — like that of the thirteenth century, under the assizes of bread and beer — during the 1960s and seventies, when it was fashionable to be ostentatiously anti-materialist. While it might be delicious to tote up how many anti-bourgeois fortunes were made on buttons, t-shirts, and rock-and-roll records endorsing peace, love, and hare Krishna, the period produced a noisy flood of trade practice legislation. Yet in the 1980s, the business ethos has become so glamorous that the most powerful nations in the world are run as though they are corporations, their "corporate philosophy" not founded in political or moral principle, but on principles of cost benefit. The workaholism and "conspicuous consumption" deplored in the sixties and seventies are now the mandatory "dressing (and eating and driving and mating) for success." In the service of this view, the constant blather about something called the "search for excellence" has acquired the insistent tone of a Newspeak propaganda slogan: anyone who thinks for a moment that this "search" has the remotest connection with truth, beauty, learning or transcendence is made to feel as ridiculous as Diogenes with his lamp, consigned in his sackcloth and ashes to the back-alleys (or dunghill) of the consumer society. The unexamined life is not only worth living, it's worth buying.

But like the protagonists of classic fiction, Ellen Donovan and Grandma Wallis, young Mrs. Donoghue and Stevenson the soda man live on, awaiting periodic resurrection, heroes of classic case law. *Donoghue* is now cited automatically, virtually every time a lawyer drafts the pleadings for a negligence or products-liability action, albeit sometimes — if the lawsuit is an attempt to soak a blameless company — in the cause of greed itself. And during those heady power-to-the-people days of 1969, its neighbor principle — that a manufacturer ought to show as much neighborly concern for the ultimate consumer two or three doors down as he does for the wholesaler and retailer right next door — was even married in a food case to the fitness principle of *Wallis*.

Presumably Edwina Martel's lawyers had decided that a straight *Donoghue v. Stevenson* negligence claim was too risky: it would have been too difficult to prove that the Duffy-Mott Corportion had been careless or reckless in respect of its Martel consumer-"neighbours." But the plain fact was that Edwina's sons, Brian, eight, and Gary, ten, had ended up in a Michigan hospital because of some Duffy-Mott applesauce, which Edwina had brought home from her local grocery store. It was clear, Edwina and the boys felt, that Duffy-Mott had breached its implied warranty to make applesauce fit for dessert.

Brian had mixed his into the rest of his food and eaten a great deal of it before his brother, who had swallowed just a spoonful or two, noticed that it "tasted funny." Edwina investigated and then phoned the hospital, who advised her to bring the children right in.

The boys gagged, and, on the way to the hospital, reported some possibly hysterical trouble breathing. After examining the applesauce, staff at the hospital decided it would be best to pump the children's stomachs. Beyond the trauma of that (the boys would describe in court how a hose had been slipped down their noses), the breathing trouble and the gagging — which Mrs. Martel admitted may have had more to do with fear than applesauce — the boys suffered no physical effects. But they stopped eating applesauce, which they had normally eaten three or four times a week, and even "shied away" from whole apples.

When, as in *Donoghue*, the defendant corporation moved for dismissal of the case before trial, the District Court of Appeals decided that Brian and Gary were "persons well experienced in eating applesauce," and therefore had a case that should go to a jury, even if the applesauce had not been poisonous. Presiding Judge Charles Levin could see no reason something inedible could be "merchantable" just because it might not physically harm the consumer, and felt that a jury should be allowed to assess that argument. In a world where power really is the purview of the people, such as the Brians and Garys who enjoy a spot of sweetened fruit of an evening, "merchantable" applesauce should be not only safe, but savory. It would be up to the plaintiffs, Judge Levin held, to convince the jury that their disgust and suffering were quantifiable in money damages.

Judges are consumers, too, of course, and while they may not be avid in great numbers for applesauce, ginger beer sodas, and Coca-Cola, their taste for the finer things can work its own influence — or so, anyway, would the Legal Realists have it. Lord Ellenborough, to return to where this chapter began, is said to have been partial to turbot with lobster sauce, a predilection that flavored his decision in a press-gang case.

His lordship was hearing an application from lobster fishermen that he should exempt them from conscription into the Royal Navy. The navy's evidence was that only deep-sea fishermen could be exempted, but the Lord Chief Justice held that this interpretation of the law was too narrow:

> Is not the lobster-fishery a fishery, and a most important fishery, of this kingdom, though carried on in shallow water? The framers of the law well know that the produce of the deep sea, without the produce of the shallow water, would be of comparatively small value, and intended that the turbot, when placed upon our tables, should be flanked by good lobster sauce.

As long as they're fit for the purpose, of course.

CHAPTER FOUR

Bosses and Workers

What Acme Steel International calls its "trade secrets," John Henry, one of Acme's foremen, might see as his special skill and knowledge, something of his own that he brings to his job. The conflict remains academic until John leaves Acme to offer his skills to Superior Metals or Supreme Alloys, or to set up as a steel-drivin' man on his own. Both he and Acme will claim a property interest in the skill and knowledge, and a struggle may ensue over John's freedom to contract with these as consideration.

If Acme sues, a court or arbitrator will be asked to determine which interests are paramount — John's freedom to work where he wishes, or the company's desire to protect itself and its other employees against loss of profit. Whose "freedom to contract" should take precedence? Indeed, what does "freedom" mean in such cases?

John does not need to leave Acme to be accused of consorting with the enemy. He can merely begin dating Jane at Superior Metals, or announce his engagement to Joan at Supreme Alloys. Acme might see such an innocent love interest as a Mata Hari, adding the sort of romance to the affair that John and Jane might only fantasize about during dull steel-drivin' moments.

In 1985, an executive with Coca-Cola was called on the carpet when her fiancé, a colleague at Coke, moved to Pepsi. According to reports in law-trade newspapers, Coke seems to have asked the woman to take a different job with them, one where she would not have access to trade secrets; the woman counters that she was given an impossible choice: quit, break her engagement or convince her fiancé to resign from Pepsi. When she demurred, her story goes, Coke fired her. There was a similar incident at IBM: the man took a job at the Qyx division of Exxon, a rival of IBM's typewriter interests, and the woman was asked to transfer to another job in IBM. A jury awarded the woman $300,000 for "constructive dismissal," including $200,000 in punitive damages. The jury agreed with her that IBM had more or less compelled her to quit by "putting her out to pasture."

Even when there are no trade secrets involved, Acme Steel may stick its nose into John Henry's bedroom, ostensibly to inquire into his suitability as an employee. They may try to impose their own morality on him, or some conventional view, arguing that sexual unconventionality might indicate other deviance, idiosyncracy, even recklessness or dishonesty. He might not be a team player.

It does not necessarily warm a boss's heart that his employees seem freer, or more sexually active than he is; indeed, it may incite retaliatory jealousy. It is a challenge, if he takes it that way, to his putative superiority, which he may attempt to reclaim by taking the moral high-ground, accusing the employees of moral "turpitude": here, the boss sets himself up as judge. His job, tacitly, is to protect the status quo, to keep the work force as predictable and manageable as the market. When his personal emotions are aroused, his job may become his excuse to repress: misery loves company.

The case law suggests that it may be safer to "moon" your boss and call him a cozening knave than to boast to him about your sexual exploits, even if the exploits are ancient history — or myth. One case in point, *Denham v. Patrick*, pitted a farm hand against his boss of nearly seven years. Patrick, a sheep rancher in Middesex County, Ontario, had grown to trust Denham, to the point that he left him in charge when he was out of town, a frequent occurrence, permitting Denham free access to Patrick's house. As part of their employment agreement, Patrick provided Denham and his family a house and one cow.

In June, 1908, Patrick remarked that he thought highly of a young woman, identified in the *Ontario Law Reports* as "Miss A." Denham replied that she was "not so fine and straight" as Patrick thought, "for he had had his hand up her clothes and on her private parts." A few days later, evidently feeling a new familiarity with his boss, Denham also bragged that he had slept with a "Miss X." before she was married.

Patrick discussed these conversations with a friend, saying he was thinking of firing Denham because of them. The friend said that Denham had told him about Miss A. during a trip to the Chicago stock yards two years earlier; it had happened, Denham had said, in Patrick's barn. This information made up Patrick's mind.

Denham denied any adultery with Miss X., and when he sued Patrick for unjustly firing him and breaking his employment contract, none was proved in court. Contesting the allegation that Miss A. had been only thirteen our fourteen at the time of the fondling (Denham said she was 22), he admitted it, but called it "accidental." In any event, it had occurred *eight years in the past*, during the first year of his service with Patrick.

Miss A. was not called as a witness. Although Denham had since proved himself a reliable employee and a law-abiding man, three judges of the Ontario Divisional Court found that he had been lawfully fired. What was decisive for Sir John Boyd, the chancellor of the province, was Denham's braggadocio: his mind "appeared to dwell with satisfaction" on the encounter with Miss A., whether or not it had really happened. It was "alike discreditable to boast of the act and disparage the woman." With a wife, three young children and a serving maid in his house, Patrick had good reason to worry whether Denham was "of lewd mind and habit." That is, he had reasonable grounds to feel that Denham's personal life could interfere with his professional one.

As the *Denham* case suggests, the employment relationship can be at least as intimate as a marriage, especially when there are problems severe enough to threaten its survival. Under stress, all the most deeply-held feelings on both sides are pressed to the surface, flotsam and jetsam of a moiling wreck in progress. But according to a prototype "wrongful dismissal" action from the beginning of the seventeenth century, extraordinary both in its facts and for its age of nearly

275 years, such expressions of anger, and even outrageous conduct on the job, will not necessarily amount to just cause for firing. Despite its age, in terms of labor relations the case seems strikingly more liberal-minded than *Denham*.

The plaintiff, James Bagg, worked as a chief burgess of Plymouth, England, a councillor, magistrate and a member of the powerful Common Council. On April 17, 1614, a majority of the other twenty-three common councillors decided that Bagg should be fired. In an affidavit to the justices who reviewed the case, Plymouth mayor John Clement recited a dozen grounds for dismissal, including sedition, breach of trust and assault, all amounting to a violation of Bagg's oath "that he should carry himself well and honestly" toward the mayor and other chief burgesses and apply himself earnestly to the community interest.

A modern reader is struck by the fact that Bagg's accusers fixed so many of his offenses, which spanned fully eleven years, on the first of the month. But perhaps these were council days or market days — or maybe expansive Bagg adhered to the old superstition, "A pinch and a punch for the first of the month." On May 1, 1608, for instance, he allegedly asked the incumbent mayor, Robert Trelawny, "You are some prince, are you not?" (the councillors were evidently so fed up with a man who never failed to speak his mind, they stretched hard to multiply examples against him) and on February 1, 1609, with like vulgarity, called Trelawny "a cozening knave." A year to the day later, he is supposed to have called Mayor John Fowens "an insolent fellow."

In a public speech on February 20, 1614, Bagg accused Clement of being a toady to King James, of "being too vigorous" in enforcing a royal decree that no meat be butchered or sold during Lent. According to the affidavit, filed with the court by Clement when Bagg sued for his job back, the speech sparked sedition among "victuallers, inn-keepers, keepers of ordinary tables, and alehouse keepers" only too happy to buck up business during the holidays.

Clement seems to have had a long, copious and very particular memory. He accused Bagg of sedition on the municipal level, as well: *eight years* before his Lent speech, Clement alleged, Bagg had "perfidiously and maliciously" divulged local budgetary information to two taverners, advising them that they did not need to pay any wine tax because the levy was extortionate. But it seems Bagg saved his most artful abuse for Mayor Fowens. On August 20, 1611, he supposedly threatened Fowens, "I will make thy neck crack," and ten days before had turned "the hinder part of his body in an inhuman and uncivil manner towards the aforesaid Thomas Fowens, [and] scoffingly, contemptuously, and uncivilly, with a loud voice, said to the aforesaid Thomas Fowens, these words following, that is to say, 'Come and kiss.'"

On April 17, 1614, finding that Bagg had ignored a common council order to "reconcile himself" to the mayor and other councillors "and faithfully promise to demean himself more orderly and temperately for the time to come," the council acted on its standing threat that Bagg be "clean removed from the Bench, and a new master chosen in his room." The recitation of complaints against him, one after another for page after page in the law reports, leaves a reader surprised at the verdict: although the court found Bagg's conduct contemptible, it held that he was wrongfully "disenfranchised." The justices were particularly concerned that Bagg's loss of civic rights would harm his innocent family and heirs. They seem, indeed, to have been more civic-minded than the civic councillors — and certainly less "business-minded" than some modern judges: only a few years ago, a U.S. District Court ruled that American Airlines was justified in firing a flight attendant for not smiling enough. The court remained unswayed by the attendant's defense of social taboo, that most of the passengers on his flights were men and "a male would resent another male smiling at him."

The court in *Bagg* admitted that, far short of express goodwill, the burgess had threatened mutiny against the corporation, and even to overthrow its charter. But he had never acted on such threats. The threats were mere words "which he may repent."

Typically, plantiffs bring trademark actions because they believe that the public will confuse the defendant's product with theirs, and that their own trademark will end up irreparably tainted or "diluted." A few years ago American Express won an injunction against an entrepreneur selling condoms in a wallet marked "Never leave home without it." And in 1987 the Mutual of Omaha insurance company stopped a peacenik from marketing T-shirts, posters, mugs and buttons printed, "Mutant of Omaha: When the world's in ashes, we'll have you covered." (The seller lived in Omaha and had chosen Mutual for its local interest and name, amenable to his political pun. Although he parodied their famous Indian-head logo by transforming it into an emaciated face in profile, he evidently was not accusing the company of promoting nuclear power or weapons; he was suggesting that "there's no insurance against nuclear holocaust.") On the other hand, in 1987, a United States Court of Appeals held that the product name "Lardashe" on the rear pocket of "husky-sized" blue jeans for women — the word being positioned under a symbolic piglet peeking over the pocket top, and above stitching shaped like a "full-figured" heart-shaped derriere — did not taint the designer trademark "Jordache."

Where a trade name is also a family name, the law has proved similarly reluctant to intervene. In *Burgess v. Burgess* in 1853, for example, two evidently identical but competing products, both called "Burgess's Essence of Anchovies," were permitted to coexist, even though the second had been snitched by a son — label, advertising and all — from a very old family recipe and business.

From a very young age, William had worked for his father in the warehouse business, and in his adulthood had been permitted to live over the premises at 107 Strand Street in London. But by the 1850s, after 30 years at John Burgess and Son, the itch to spread his wings became irresistible. It was time, he told John, to strike out in business on his own.

John soon discovered that the signs on William's new shop breezily proclaimed, "Burgess's Fish Sauce Warehouse, late of 107 Strand," and that William was selling as his own an anchovy sauce that, on the label, anyway, seemed a lot like "Burgess's Essence of Anchovies," a condiment John had always made and sold based on a recipe handed down from Grandfather John. John II's label had always said,

Original and Superior Essence of Anchovies. The excellence of their much esteemed essence of anchovies stands unrivalled as a fish sauce, viz., for salmon, turbot, soles, eels, cod, haddock, and in all stewed fish. Burgess's New Sauce is strongly recommended to those palates not partial to anchovy.

William's label read,

> Burgess's Essence of Anchovies. The excellence of the much
> esteemed essence of anchovies, stands unrivalled as a fish sauce,
> viz., for salmon, turbot, soles, eels, cod, and for all stewed fish.
> Burgess's Universal Sauce is confidently recommended to those not
> partial to the essence of anchovies.

At trial, John was awarded an injunction restraining William from
using "late of 107 Strand" and from advertising "Burgess's Fish Sauce
Warehouse, late of 107 Strand" on his door, but William was permitted to continue marketing his anchovy sauce, seemingly compounded according to the old family recipe owned by his father,
without interference. John appealed to the Court of Queen's Bench,
but Lord Justice James Knight-Bruce held that the "celebrity" of John's
sauce did not "give him such exclusive right, such a monopoly, such
a privilege, as to prevent any [other] man from making essence of
anchovies, and selling it under his own name" — even if that name
happened to be Burgess as well. "All the Queen's subjects have the
right, if they will, to manufacture and sell pickles and sauces, and
not the less that their fathers have done so before them."

Historically, the courts have refused to enforce putative contracts
among relatives: even at law, blood is supposed to be thicker than
the scotch-and-water that lubricates an employment relationship or
closes a business deal. Unless a litigant produces strong evidence that
all parties envisaged a really binding agreement from the outset, the
courts have often assumed that among relatives, promises are now
and then made to be broken.

Again, this may have less to do with the realities of everyday life
than with the fact that the judges who make such confident pro-
nouncements have tended to be male, white, middle-class, middle-
aged, and fretfully conservative — people who don't necessarily need
to sue a spouse for grocery or day-care money. In any case, the Burgess
family tiff over anchovy sauce may simply be one of those "hard cases"
that, as the lawyer's truism has it, "make bad law." It is an extreme
example (and was soon overturned, albeit on the unsupported ground
that the two sauces were much different), inexplicable really, beyond
psychoanalytic speculation. It has the uncomfortable feel about it

of a bunch of old men reliving their salad days by ganging up with a willful Oedipus against his father. Maybe some visceral or "Freudian" sympathy with William Burgess that, yes, he *should* make a life separate from his father's, discouraged the judges from intervening completely in favor of father over son. Maybe in some usually hidden depths, some judges really do believe that the old order, like the Fisher King, must give way eventually to the new.

The 1934 case of Albert Edward Hall, while fairer on the evident equities, proves further that there need not be a family relationship between litigants for a man to trade on his birthright. Hall was leader of what he called the Albert Hall Orchestra, which he hired out to theaters, hotels and clubs. The officers of the London Hall of Arts and Sciences, more commonly known as the Albert Hall, seemed to believe that Albert Hall, the person, was taking advantage of the nominal coincidence to make the public think that his orchestra and the Hall of Arts and Sciences were affiliated.

Mr. Hall denied doing anything other than answering to his own name, which prompted Albert Hall, the institution, to ask why, then, he couldn't call his group "Albert Hall's Orchestra." Justice A.C. Clauson of the Court of Chancery scoffed at Hall's reply that "Albert Hall's Orchestra" sounded down-market from the Albert Hall Orchestra. But the judge found it hard to believe that the orchestra as named would damage the hall's business, as the hall did not "hire out orchestral performances to theatres, hotels and clubs." They and Albert Edward could not be called "competitors." The Albert Hall's application for an injunction against Albert E. Hall's use of his name was denied.

Indeed, even if a name is not congenitally your own, you may have special rights in it against an employer. In 1908, for example, Gertrude Landa successfully claimed property rights against the *Jewish Chronicle* newspaper in the pseudonym "Aunt Naomi." Mrs. Landa had written a column for the *Chronicle* called, at first, "The Children's Corner, Conducted by Aunt Naomi," and later, "Aunt Naomi's Chat." When she wrote an article under her real name for the *Daily News*, the editor at the *Chronicle* objected and peremptorily fired her — evidently because she had consorted with the competition. But he continued to use the "Aunt Naomi" name in some of the *Chronicle*'s publicity.

Justice H.T. Eve of the Court of Chancery held that "Aunt Naomi" was part of Mrs. Landa's "stock-in-trade as a writer," her private property: "that it had become identified with her was the very reason the defendant [the *Jewish Chronicle*] put forward for dismissing her." The *Chronicle* was forbidden to use "Aunt Naomi" and ordered to pay Mrs. Landa thirty pounds in lieu of notice of dismissal.

Nearly forty years later, *Landa* was cited with approval in *Hines v. Winnick,* litigation over the title "Dr. Crock and His Crackpots." Hines had become Dr. Crock when hired as musical director and performer on a BBC radio program called "Ignorance Is Bliss." Not surprisingly, he was at first dismayed that, as a professional musician of some repute, his own name was thought less attractive than "Dr. Crock." Yet within a few weeks, he had made a hit as Dr. Crock, and his picture had appeared under that name in the English press, which gave his Dr. Crock character laudatory reviews.

Winnick, the executive producer of "Ignorance Is Bliss," claimed that Dr. Crock was a fictional character separate from Hines, and that any musical director hired for "Ignorance Is Bliss" could be given that name. (A Hollywood producer could cite precedent for this in "The Three Stooges" movies, where the "Curly" character was played by several actors.) Hines countered that he and Crock had become identified as one person.

Winnick admitted to the Court of Chancery that "if, for instance, he was told that Duke Ellington and his orchestra were to perform, he would expect the gentleman known as Duke Ellington to be the conductor of it." In response, the court ruled that, as with "Aunt Naomi" in the *Landa* case, "Dr. Crock" had become part of the plaintiff's stock in trade. At the same time, Justice Harry Vaisey did not think that Hines had "any right to a monopoly in the use of the word 'Crackpots.'"

But then, he didn't know that Hines had "any monopoly in the use of the words 'Dr. Crock,'" either, though he felt "bound to say that applicants for the privilege of using that name are unlikely to be very numerous or insistent."

The sorest incident to the employment relationship is probably the corollary "social contract" between workers and the revenue department of their governments. Indeed, government involvement is so intrusive here that its interaction with the working person often amounts to a powerful method of social control. Still, while Big Brother may be watching, the literature and case law on income taxation suggests that there is a lot he doesn't see. History consistently shows what is now a given in sociology: where there is community responsibility, individuals may come to feel that their own contribution is unnecessary, especially if that contribution might cause them individual discomfort. Somebody else, they tell themselves, will take up the slack. More bluntly said, efforts to avoid paying one's share will always prove more creative than any attempt to frustrate them.

In the early 1980s, something like $60 billion in income went untaxed in Canada, partly because men coming through customs ostentatiously subscribed, at least for the purposes of crossing the border, to the love that dare not speak its name. (Customs duties are taxes on imported goods.) Word on the streets had it, evidently, that customs officers shied away from dealing with the sexually unconventional, even short of body-searches and well before anyone had heard of the AIDS virus. For more reasons than one, out of sight, out of mind might well have been a smuggler's (and customs officer's) anthem.

Less venturesome, but no less artful, cynics have enclosed a shirt with their annual income-tax forms, presumably the very one off their backs, sweat-soaked from an all-nighter over the calculator. Others have gone so far as to electrify doorknobs, to discourage visits by field auditors. And then there are those who simply don't bother to file, the commonest (and stupidest) form of tax evasion.

If tax evasion rivals hockey as the national pastime, it is the government's own fault. Tax officials have become so phobic about evasion, a recent book says, that they have overreacted, making the *Income Tax Act* inscrutable with that fear and thereby making the fear into a self-fulfilling reality. By preferring income tax to other methods of raising revenue (such as user-pay commodity taxes), government has asked the ordinary working person to bear too much of the national debt; and it has been too ferocious in pursuing these "little guys," finding them easier marks than fat-cat corporations with their Byzantine accounting methods.

Shrewder citizens, or those who can afford savvy consultants, try to skirt the margin of evasion with "tax avoidance." Legendary among revenuers, evidently, is the pizza entrepreneur who wrote to an auditor, "You asked me to explain how five trips to Italy could be a business expense for the restaurant. Very simple. We deliver." A well-known tax expert has recommended, with his tongue not altogether in his cheek, that taxpayers marry with an eye to amassing deductions, the "perfect tax spouse" having been at the time (in Canada) a student older than sixty-five who was crippled or blind and who made $1,000 a year in investment income and $1,000 in pension income.

As chronicled in A.P. Herbert's *Uncommon Law*, especially well-named in this instance, in the 1950s the irrepressible Albert Haddock did convince Mr. Justice Radish that, insofar as all life is grist for the mill, a writer might legally claim a tax deduction for *all* his costs of living, including trips to Monte Carlo, champagne, nightclub expenses (otherwise, how could he write about these things?), and the consequent wear and tear on his body and brain. For an author, all trips were business trips, all consumption necessary to fuel his business enterprise, all movement and thought "wear and tear of machinery and plant."

Unfortunately, in the cold light of a real courtroom no less imaginative arguments have failed. In Britain during World War II, a court stenographer who fell ill, ostensibly because of unhealthy conditions in the justice buildings, strenuously pressed a claim for deductions under the "wear and tear of plant" section of the British *Income Tax Act*. Perhaps inspired by the advocacy he had witnessed during working hours, he led clear evidence of lost work time and medical expenses. While Lord Greene was sympathetic, especially insofar as businessmen and tradesmen were usually accorded more tax breaks than "professional men" like court clerks, he held that "your own body is not plant." A horse might be plant, or at least a horse had been held a plant under the *Employer's Liability Acts*, Lord Greene admitted, but no one had ever held a person to be plant.

According to the study of the Canadian situation, so widespread are efforts to dodge income taxation that it must be viewed as a form of political protest. Indeed, the American and French revolutions, the book suggests, can be seen as "tax revolts that got out of hand." But even assuming the ordinary taxpayer is genuinely a political animal, this conclusion seems romantic: on the same logic, bank robberies and extortion could be revolutionary, every crook a Robin Hood or Jean Valjean. History's most prominent tax evaders, after all, have not been disgruntled John Publics and Jane Does, but those with the biggest vested interests in the status quo, those already so enveloped in self-interest that it never occurs to them that they have a moral duty (and a solemn obligation under the social contract) to share the cost of government and community services with the ordinary solid citizen. Al Capone, to take an example the book's authors cite more than once — and who, they point out, was finally corralled not for murder or bootlegging but tax fraud — may have been a non-conformist, but he was no utopian ideologue.

Still, occasionally reason can rear up through the looking-glass, be it reason of a looking-glass kind. For example, the Federal Court of Canada has held that workers can deduct fines for traffic violations from their taxes; the only prerequisite is that the fines be an unavoidable incident of business or employment. (The business in the case at bar was trucking.) In both the United States and Canada, employers have been allowed to deduct losses they suffered from pilfering by employees. (The logic is, again, that pilfering is an unavoidable incident of business. The same may not be true of embezzlement, the reasoning being that because it is a white-collar crime, it is more unusual and more easily avoidable.) But if an employer gives an honest employee a small bonus — something that a less scrupulous worker might abscond with as a self-awarded "perk" of the job — the employee will be dunned for the bonus by the tax man. In Britain in 1961, a court ordered a man to pay income tax on a suit of clothing his employer gave him, unasked, at Christmastime, even though the garment's resale value was a mere five pounds, and it had been tailored specifically to the taxpayer's physique.

But the wages of sin are deductible even when the taxpayer is a madam (or pimp or gangster) who argues, reasonably, that it would be incongruous and hypocritical for the government to assess her because then they, too, would be living off the avails of prostitution. That argument failed to impress the Exchequer Court of Canada in 1964 (as well as courts in Britain during the 1980s), although taxpayer Olva Eldridge was allowed many deductions, including legal fees and money for strong-arm men.

Her operation was sophisticated, with nine full-time employees, two dispatchers and seven prostitutes. Its sophistication, in fact, lubricated its downfall, detailed call sheets having been seized by police and turned over to tax inspectors. In business from 1953, Eldridge began filing returns in 1957, when, according to Exchequer Justice Angus Cattanach, tax officials "pointed out the advantages and necessity of maintaining complete records." At issue were claims pertaining to taxation years 1959 and 1960, during which Eldridge had grossed, at the very least, $77,661 and $80,749 — very high income for the time. Revenuers had allowed her more than $53,000 in tax deductions for 1959 and almost $60,000 for 1960 — "salaries," commissions, telephone costs, room rentals, refreshments, taxis, bad debts. When the tax-appeal board allowed her deductions of another $11,860 and $9,700 for those years, the Minister of Revenue appealed to the courts.

Justice Cattanach affirmed the appeal board's allowance of deductions for room rentals ($1,925) and lawyers' and bodyguard fees ($100), and $5,400 in bail-bond commissions Eldridge had paid to get her girls out of the slammer. (His lordship saw such a service as part of Eldridge's "contractual obligations" as an employer.) But because Eldridge did not produce receipts, she could not claim

— $1,000 supposedly paid to a moonlighting telephone-company serviceman who checked her phones for wiretaps;
— $16,750 ostensibly paid to the police as "protection money";
— $4,600 allegedly provided, in the form of liquor, to city government panjandrums;
— more than $4,300 in rent and utility bills;
— nearly $1,700 supposedly paid to "casual employees" for a "Penthouse party";
— $500 expended to buy up an entire print run of a sensationalist newspaper that described Eldridge as "a Czarina of the underworld" with enemies who "subjected her to loathsome indignities" (charges strenuously denied by the taxpayer before the tax-appeal board);
— $1,000 paid in commission to a bail bondsman to secure the taxpayer's own freedom.

The Exchequer Court would have allowed this last item as a legitimate business expense had Eldridge not been run directly out of business near the time of that transaction, upon being convicted of living off the avails of prostitution. Catch-22 proved operative, though it went under a different name and number in the *Income Tax Act.*

Among the cases concerning on-the-job injuries, two American instances stand out both on their facts and for the way they seem to have tickled a judicial hankering for rhetorical flight. Spectacular accident becomes the occasion for cracker-barrel humor — an old literary trick, of course, but one that must be played with extreme caution in the courtroom.

The conventional rationalization for such jocularity is the Freudian one: courtroom laughter is cathartic, an antidote to the tedium and tragedy so commonly rehearsed there. But such cliché excuses betray an unnecessary attack of conscience. Often, by the time some genuine disaster reaches trial or appeal, years after its occurrence, every detail has been analyzed and rehashed by expert witnesses, lawyers, and judges, to the point that it has become completely abstracted, even "metaphysical." Irony and coincidence take on a surreal prominence — as, for example, in the case of a mugging reported in the New York *Times* in 1986, during which two men dressed as women stabbed a priest on the subway. When attacked, the priest, en route to visit his sick father, was reading the book *When Bad Things Happen to Good People.*

Of course it wasn't funny at the time. In the recounting, even of such cases as a woman beating her husband to death with his artificial arm, or the Frenchman killed in 1979 when his peers in group therapy placed him between two mattresses and "walked over him to stamp out his complexes," calamity has a fictive, climactic quality, an unusual way of throwing everything into relief, making daily life seem more exciting and instructive than it might otherwise be. Judicial humor is generally not at a litigant's expense, but arises out of the fact that the calamity under minute inspection is some distillation of the tragedy and tedium of the greater Human Comedy. A victim or plaintiff becomes a protagonist, larger than life like the hero of a novel; by the time his case is concluded, his name may represent some legal principle or notion (the "*Miranda* warning," the "*Donoghue v. Stevenson* neighbor principle") just as the names of fictional characters can represent ideas and philosophies (a "Walter Mitty sort of person," a "Babbit," a "Madame Bovary"). As the evidence unfolds, it can seem as though no honest bone was broken, no sanguine flesh torn and rent, as though all those in the courtroom, even those who have suffered the most from the events, are watching their own movie, sometimes a Harold Lloyd or Charlie Chaplin movie, where bad things happen to good people, but nobody seems really to get hurt.

Thus, when Armin Vann accused Rose Ionta of employing a barber who had "an unusual propensity for fooling around with customers," Justice Nicholas Pette could not resist the temptation to fashion his opinion as an excursus on the legacy of Figaro.

The case itself was simple. Jimmie the barber testified that by 1935 he had been in the business ten years and that it was not his professional habit to poke clients like Armin Vann in the ribs, let alone tickle them. Vann must have become ticklish, Jimmie figured, when Jimmie went to wipe his razor on the sheet over his customer's chest, causing Vann to grab the razor and cut himself seriously enough that fourteen stitches were taken in his hand.

Jimmie had shaved Vann, who ran a business in the neighborhood, twice before, to Vann's satisfaction. This time, Vann claimed, Jimmie told him jokes and tickled him until he couldn't stop and lost all control of himself — to the point that he fell out of the barber chair. That was why he had thoughtlessly grabbed the razor.

On the theory that an employer is liable for the acts of her servant (at least insofar as the servant causes harm in the normal performance of his duties), Vann sued Ionta, who owned the barbershop. She was negligent, Vann claimed before the New York Municipal Court in Queens, to employ someone with this abnormal "propensity" for fooling around.

Justice Pette's judgment is virtually all *obiter dicta*, erudite asides on the history of barbering, irrelevant to the legal issues. His research, his honor writes, convinced him that it had always been central to a barber's job description that he be an entertainer — or, as Jimmie put it when Judge Pette asked him if he wasn't trespassing on the turf of Eddie Cantor, "Well, when a customer comes in he doesn't like to sit in the chair and be still, he wants you to talk to him."

Throughout history, Justice Pette found, barbershops were as much social clubs, when not surgeries, as tonsorial parlors. Historically, the barber was "the original newspaper"; in Italy, "the index of publicity was whether a subject had been discussed in a barbershop." Barbers were *expected* to be philosophical, garrulous, obliging, "always dispensing vocal wares with varying degrees of humor and intelligence, while the razor follows the facial contours and, maybe, the course of least resistance, depending upon when it was last sharpened. That barbers talk cannot be disputed. It is traditional and hereditary with them."

Justice Pette's efforts to exculpate Jimmie ranged so far and wide that *Vann v. Ionta* may be the only case report that includes the libretto, personalized and abridged, of an opera, or at least of *The Barber of Seville*. ("That Figaro acquits himself nobly in all his missions demonstrates that the present barber's predecessor was a genial and astute fellow with courageous directness, witty lies, proverbial shrewdness, and a somewhat charmed life.")

To a large extent, then, by taking the barber's chair, a customer voluntarily put himself at risk, in the hands of a stranger wielding a blade at his jugular, "for well may he recall, before he engages in conversation, the words of Dante upon entering Inferno, 'Abandon all hope all ye who enter here.' " But the justice found that the injury to Armin Vann was an "unavoidable accident." Neither Jimmie nor Rose was liable for Vann's hurt hand. A "propensity to fool around," like the pseudonym of a writer or musician, was part of a barber's lawful stock in trade.

Finally, the 1948 New York case, *Koistinen v. American Export Lines*, concerns injury to an employee himself, raising the nice question whether a worker who courts disaster can claim compensation. It demonstrates, as well, that since World War II, it has become more difficult for employers to avoid provisions of employment contracts by impugning a worker's private "moral turpitude." Even in contract law, sexuality has come out of the closet since the days of *Denham v. Patrick*.

On shore leave in Yugoslavia from his duties as fireman and coaltender on the SS *John N. Robins*, Eino Koistinen had met a woman in a bar "whose blandishments," according to New York City Court Justice Frank Carlin, "lured him to the room for purposes not particularly platonic." It turned out that Koistinen's spirit was more than willing but his flesh wasn't up to it, so, on the basis of nonperformance — albeit his own — he refused to pay. Though the prostitute insisted on her "dinner" ("the court erroneously interpreted the word as showing that the woman had a carnivorous frenzy which could only be soothed by the succulent sirloin provided at the plaintiff's expense"), Koistinen remained adamant.

Of course, if sex for money had been a lawful enterprise, the prostitute could have staked a solid legal claim on the contract. Forced to resort to her own manner of enforcement, she tried to take the money from Koistinen, but failing at that, locked him in her room. Koistinen kicked at the door without success and had gone to the window, which was between six and eight feet from the ground, when another man "formidably loomed at the lintels" of the door, armed with a knife. Koistinen jumped out the window.

He sustained injuries that put him in the hospital in Yugoslavia, then in the United States. But when he sought compensation, his employer, American Export Lines, argued that his "immoral intent" nullified their obligation to pay; randiness, not anything legitimately covered by his contract of employment, was the true "proximate cause" of his fall — or leap — from grace.

Four years earlier, Lord Justice Du Parcq had summed up the usual dangers of wandering into the legal thicket of causation in situations like this. In a case about a coke worker who fell to his death from an unfenced, unlighted catwalk, his lordship said: "Unless the trial had taken place in a university city and it had happened that the jury was composed mainly of philosophers and logicians, I doubt if a discussion of theories of causation would have either assisted or interested them."

If, for example, a tenant habitually uses a privy with an obviously rotted trapdoor and one day falls through the trap into the muck below (nine feet by her testimony, nine inches by her landlord's), is she negligent, and therefore the proximate cause of her own injury, or is her landlord to blame? (The Supreme Court of New Jersey held that the woman had no choice "when impelled by the calls of nature, but to use the facilities placed at her disposal," and refused the landlord's request to dismiss the suit before a jury decided the issue. In other words, the argument that the landlord was the "proximate cause" was a legitimate issue: the jury would make up its own mind. Presumably it would do the same on whether a ladder had been required to extricate the woman from her misfortune.)

Again, what if Private Creed is stabbed in the back with a bayonet during a drunken brawl and his colleagues drop him twice while carrying him to the doctor? What if so many people are hurt in the fight that the medics give Creed oxygen and artificial respiration, then leave him on intravenous saline while they tend to those they think are more seriously injured? Who is most directly to blame if it turns out that Creed's lung has been pierced and he dies, compressed oxygen and artificial respiration only hastening death in such cases? The stabber? The besotted rescuers? The overwhelmed medics?

(The English Court of Queen's Bench convicted the stabber of murder: the wound itself was so serious, they held, that it continued to be an "operating and substantial cause" throughout that horrible night, no matter what happened subsequently.)

In the coke worker case, the court ruled that the man's failure to use a flashlight or lamp made him at least one proximate cause of his own death; despite the unsafe conditions he worked under, his widow could not recover compensation. In Koistinen's case, Justice Carlin admitted that the sailor had not gone to the prostitute's room "for heavenly contemplation," but held that the "ticklish situation" he found himself in just before his defenestration "was not a reasonably foreseeable consequence of his original situation." He had not been negligent in seeking the woman's services. The proximate cause of his injuries was not the visit to the brothel, but "the concurrence of the locked door . . . and the subsequent looming threat of the man with the menacing mien."

While the law would disallow maintenance to sailors who contracted venereal diseases, injured themselves while drunk or were otherwise reckless or indiscreet, it did not inquire into the morality of their behavior during the shore-leave portion of their employment. Shore leave was part of the sailor's contract, and Koistinen was entitled to worker's compensation: sailors, after all, will be boys — an allowance, as we have seen, not accorded landlubbers such as ranch-hands. The life of a sailor was unusually stressful and, according to the common law, seamen were "wards of the court" to be "treated with the tenderness of a guardian."

CHAPTER FIVE

Ratepayers and Renters

Death has always played a prominent role in the common law of real estate. In Anglo-Saxon times, by inheriting real property — or simply by enjoying a right of inheritance to it in the future — a citizen acquired immediate equity and status. As the Crown turned more and more land over to private management during the Middle Ages, land conveyance being the way the king paid for services from the tenants, the value of such inheritances increased dramatically. Before that, if you were unlanded, your worth was restricted pretty much to your incorporeal soul. A money economy took shape only after mediaeval kings had parceled out virtually all of Britain.

The word "mortgage" itself is from the Norman French for "dead pledge," and carries a common mediaeval notion that the land had a life so long as whoever held title to it put it to some productive use. There existed an almost animistic respect for real estate, perhaps a subconscious homage to ancient times, when the earth and sky were deities whose intercourse literally bore fruit. According to Lord Coke, chief justice, attorney general, and a contemporary of Shakespeare who was the first to codify English law in a comprehensive way (he also prosecuted the man thought to be the model for wealthy land-holder Shylock in *The Merchant of Venice*), land became "dead" to buyers (mortgagors) if they did not make timely payment; that is, the seller took it back. If the mortgagors paid, the debt became "dead" to the seller once the money changed hands. By the Middle Ages, "gage" itself had become an English word, synonymous with our "deposit," pledge money you had to forfeit if you broke a promise. Putting up "gage money" was one way you could "wage your law" under the old ecclesiastical and early common-law trial procedure.

The idea of "mortmain" took hold at the same time, soon after the Norman Conquest, with the notion that, unless the Crown got its full share of takings "incident" to some real estate, the property was in a "dead hand" (the literal translation from the French). Usually, land was said to be mortmain if it was held by a church or other "unproductive" charitable institution. Under many "spiritual tenures," the tenants, usually monks, nuns or other divines, were required to do little more than pray for the souls of the landlord or king and his heirs. Under the tenure called *frankalmoign* ("free alms"), the obligation was so light that even the number and occasion of the prayers were not specified.

In one form or another, Britain retained mortmain laws for nearly seven hundred years, and versions of them have cropped up from time to time in North America. The notion of mortmain persists in the sense that churches are still permitted to hold real estate tax-free. And there is one case on the books in which property was held by a dead hand in a graphically literal fashion. It came to light in 1652, when Howell Gwinn was convicted in England of forging a deed. Like many people who assume the law is mostly loophole, Gwinn had evidently thought he would be safe on a technicality. His defense was that he had seen the deed executed by the hand of another — the hand of the dead man who had owned the land. In fact, he had cut the hand off the corpse, put a pen and seal in it, "and so signed, sealed, and delivered" the property over to himself "and swore that he saw the deed sealed and delivered." Chief Justice Roll fined him one hundred pounds and ordered him to stand in the pillory for two hours "with a paper on your head, shewing the nature of your offence."

More mundane tenures — contracts for goods and services in exchange for land — ranged from the cold-bloodedly pragmatic to the picayune (for the king's needs were numberless) to the whimsical. Four "bondmen," for example, were rewarded with a messuage (a house with the surrounding buildings and land) "by the service of making the Gallowes and hanging the Theeves," as well as plowing, reaping, making "the Lords malt," and other menial jobs. A farmer in Yorkshire owed his landlord "a Snowball at Midsummer, and a Red Rose at Christmas" — which, in an age unassisted by refrigeration and greenhouses, was perhaps not so frivolous after all.

Tenures called "serjeanty" involved direct service to the king, "keeping the Gaol of the County of Exter," "weighing the Money coming from the Exchequer" and "finding footmen with bows and arrows." And because rest and recreation were important to the armed forces then as now, John Warbleton held the manor of Shirefield, in the County of Southampton "by the Grand Serjeanty, viz., by the Service of being Marshall of the Whores" — an arrangement known, according to one commentator, as "Pimp Tenure." Warbleton was evidently a fun-loving fellow, for, beyond providing sexual catharsis to the armed forces, his sergeanty required "dismembering Condemned Malefactors, and measuring the Gallons and Bushels in the King's Household."

Holding things for the king was a common condition of serjeanty. The Prioress of St. Leonard of Stretford was tenant of fifty acres in Middlesex for "finding for the Lord the King a man to hold the Towel of the same King at his Coronation." William fitz Warin was accorded an entire third of a town in Northampton for holding the king's stirrup on his birthday; and Solomon de Campis worked land in Kent on the condition that he held the king's *head* whenever the sovereign made the sea journey between Dover and Whitsond.

Rowland le Sarcere held a hundred and ten acres in Suffolk as long as he performed every Christmas for the king "*unum Saltum, unum Sufflum, et unum Bombulum*" simultaneously. This has been variously translated as "a Leap, a Puff, and a Fart," "he shall dance, puff up his Cheeks, making therewith a sound, and let a Crack," and, in not-exactly-law French, "un Saut, un Pet, et un Syflet." Indeed, real humiliation was sometimes the obvious end of tenure obligations, or remedy for breach of them. In Somersetshire, one widow held land on a manor only until she married or was "found incontinent," but she could pay penance for any incontinency and repossess her property

> if she come into the next Court, riding astride upon a Ram, and in open Court do say to the Lord, if he be present, or to his Steward, these words:
>> For mine Arse's Fault take I this Pain,
>> Therefore, my Lord, give me my Land again.

Though true feudal incidents became antiquated at home and sat badly with the rising spirit of New World independence, the English Crown attempted to transfer the tenure system to the colonies. The land granted by the Crown to Lord Baltimore in what is now Maryland was held under charter for "two Indian arrows from those parts to be delivered every year on Tuesday in Easter Week." Pennsylvania was rented annually to the colonists for the bargain-basement quit-rent of two beaver skins. The Crown's advantage in such deals was still profound: it exercised sovereignty over the colonies with these yearly reminders reinforcing the daily ones having to do with colonial government and taxes; and if in a material sense the "rent" due was trifling, it was thereby perhaps calculated to keep down seditious rumbling, at least among colonists who cared more about money and goods than symbols. The lion need only wrinkle its nose to remind us who is boss.

By the time of the Old West, most tenancy arrangements required the renter to pay in money or goods, and penalties for breach could have a piquant frontier flavor. If, for instance, a traveler didn't pay his rent on a room for the night, the innkeeper had a lien on his horse, and could keep it until the traveler paid what was owed. In the mid-1800s, one innkeeper was fined for obstructing the mails when he seized some horses which belonged to carriers for the Pony Express. Indeed, so adamant was the United States government about moving the mail no matter what, that in 1868 a Kentucky sheriff was charged with obstructing the mail because he arrested a murderer while the criminal was performing his day job as a postal-carrier. The sheriff, however, was acquitted, although the judge who let him off seems to have been hopelessly confused about who was wearing the black and who the white ten-gallon hats. In exculpating the sheriff from any wrongdoing, he said the law did not intend absurd results: it would never blame "a prisoner who breaks out when the prison is on fire — 'for he is not to be hanged because he would not stay to be burnt.'"

A landlord's obligations often reach beyond providing land and buildings, of course. As the New Jersey "proximate cause" case in the last chapter shows, he may be liable for injuries a tenant sustains on rented property — when, for instance, she falls into a privy through a rotted floor.

In 1948, the posh St. Francis Hotel in San Francisco was sued by Beulah Larson after she had been knocked unconscious by an overstuffed armchair careering from the hotel window. The chair had evidently been jettisoned as part of a celebration of V-J Day. But the California justice system did not allow Larson to recover against the hotel, because the St. Francis did not have "exclusive control" of the chair. If she could have determined who threw it, or even who was renting the room and hosting the wild party, she might have succeeded against one or both of them. But the hotel owners and management could not have "reasonably foreseen" that some nut would act in such a thoughtless way (a more reasonable proposition, perhaps, than the one in *Koistinen*, which held that the sailor could not have reasonably foreseen that he risked bodily harm when he went to a brothel). The court distinguished the case from one in which a hotel guest was beaned by falling ceiling plaster, ceiling disintegration being something the hotel could have foreseen and controlled.

In *Sayers v. Harlow Urban District Council*, injuries were again sustained in a toilet, a public one. Mr. and Mrs. Sayers were awaiting a bus to London, due in twenty minutes, when Mrs. Sayers went to spend a penny. Once inside the pay toilet, she discovered that the door, which was seven feet high, was missing its interior handle. There was no attendant, so Mrs. Sayers tried to work the lock with her fingers.

Finding that this failed and beginning to feel desperate, she attempted to reach her hand through the window above her head to signal someone. This also proved impossible, so she banged on the stall door and shouted for help. Finally, realizing that her bus was due in about five minutes, "with skirts and, no doubt, high heels," as her lawyer put it, Mrs. Sayers tried to climb over the door by putting her left foot on the toilet seat and her right foot on the toilet-roll fixture.

When this would not work, either, she began to clamber down, resting her weight on the toilet-paper roller, at which time, as Justice Francis Evershed of the Court of Appeal explained, "the toilet roll, true to its mechanical requirements, rotated, and that unfortunately disturbed her equilibrium."

Mrs. Sayers's action was framed in the tort of negligence, but could derive in part from a contractual duty owed the public by the council and its train station. In fact, "spending a penny" turns a call of nature into a contract and implies that the spender should be able to transact her business in reasonable safety. The district council argued that the lack of a handle on the door was not a proximate cause of her fall. But Lord Evershed, speaking for the three-judge panel, disagreed. When "a woman goes to a public lavatory and finds that she is immured in it, it seems to me to be asking too much of the so-called reasonable man or woman to suppose that he or she would just remain inactive." All the same, his lordship held the district council only three-quarters liable, assessing twenty-five percent of the blame to Mrs. Sayers.

"Frustration" has a more technical meaning in contract law, one that landlord-tenant cases have helped shape. An agreement is frustrated in the legal sense if its performance is made impossible by some event outside the control of the parties — war, for example, or, as in one famous case, the burning down of a concert hall where a singer was to perform. The impresarios who had organized the concert sued the hall management, but were refused damages because an intervening event outside the control of all parties had frustrated (and thus nullified) the hall-rental deal. The fire was not the impresarios' fault, but neither could it be blamed on the defendant building managers.

A wide assortment of frustration claims cropped up in 1902, once the coronation of Queen Victoria's son Edward had to be postponed when the new king fell ill. The most widely reported suit was filed by Paul Krell, who had put up a sign in the window of his London offices, offering his view of Pall Mall at seventy-five pounds to anyone who wanted to watch the coronation parade.

C.S. Henry had applied to rent the rooms and windows and paid a deposit. When the coronation was canceled a day before the parade was supposed to take place, he refused to pay the rent. Krell sued, arguing that it seemed unfair that he should bear the loss for something he had no control over. He had given up the right to rent the rooms to anyone else during the two days Henry had wanted them. It was unjust, he said, to make him an "insurer" of Henry's unspoken "hopes and expectations"; if that was to be doctrine in contract law, the economy would end up a shambles, promisors always carrying the entire risk that some vague desire of the promisee would be frustrated by a catastrophe unforeseen by anyone.

The concert-hall case, Krell's lawyer said, applied only when the subject of the contract was physically eradicated, making "performance" impossible in the most literal sense. Here, "performance" was still possible; the rooms and windows continued to exist, and Henry could have used them as much as he liked. Whether a parade passed or failed to pass was not Krell's concern.

But the courts agreed with Henry's lawyer: implied in the rental agreement, at the very heart of it, was the stipulation that there would be a coronation parade. It was irrelevant that neither Henry nor Krell's solicitor had mentioned the parade in closing the deal for the rooms. It was not like the hypothetical case, raised by the solicitor, of someone hiring a cab at an enhanced price to get to the Epsom races only to find that they were canceled. The passenger would still owe the fare insofar as the cab had no particular qualifications over any other cab, whereas Krell's Pall Mall windows were especially suited for an event the world witnessed only once or twice in a person's lifetime.

Similar complications arose in other "coronation cases," involving the hiring of rooms, viewing stands, ships (for viewing or participating in a "naval review" associated with the festivities) and the like, where large sums of money, sometimes the whole contract price, had been paid before Edward became ill. In line with *Krell*, the courts took the easy road, saying that the "loss lay where it fell" at the time of frustration: if money had been paid or was payable before the coronation was called off, the renter could not recover or avoid paying it.

For the next forty years, a promisor who was paid in advance could go back on his word with impunity, and 100 percent profit, simply by crying "Frustration!" Eventually, sense prevailed and losses were more often shared; the promisee became liable only for money spent or work done by the promisor before frustration.

Modern agreements of purchase and sale have enlarged the glossary of "mortgage," "mortmain" and of the various sorts of tenures. The most colorful addition, perhaps, is "gazump," which became a lawyers' word by way of a real-estate boom in Britain during the sixties and seventies. In that context, it was applied where a buyer agreed to sell his house to Black for one price but then, before any contract was signed, sold the house to White for a higher price.

Until Parliament intervened, a lot of home buyers got gazumped, which made the term seem just minted. But under "gazoomph," the Oxford English Dictionary gives printed usages since 1928:

> *Daily Express* 19 Dec. 2/7 'Gazoomphing the sarker' is a method of parting a rich man from his money. An article is auctioned over and over again, and the money bid each time is added to it.

In 1971, the *Guardian* reported that "gazump" came from "car trade slang for selling to one buyer and then, as values rise, to a second buyer." Among sharps and shysters, it had long been shorthand for "double-dealing."

Folk etymology says the word's origin is Yiddish, but it is more likely oafish mimicry of Yiddish. Leo Rosten, author of *The Joy of Yiddish* and *Horray for Yiddish* writes, "My experts do not give any Yiddish cognate for *gazoomph*. There's a Yiddish *gozlen* (robber, bandit) which, as a verb, means to plunder. I suspect English cockneys coined *gazoomph*."

Just seven years ago, the Ontario Court of Appeal broke linguistic ground by holding that "any defined space" — including a parking lot, bare asphalt painted with parallel lines — could be a common bawdy house. Such a "house" did not need to be covered or enclosed as long as prostitution had been taking place within a "substantial" portion of it.

The inspiration for this unusual philology was an indictment against two women charged with being "keepers" of a particular stretch of asphalt in downtown Toronto, and "common" seems a fair description of an otherwise nocturnal no-person's-land behind a building in the seedier reaches of Richmond Street. The Crown alleged that the women would approach johns in their cars at other locations on nearby streets, then accompany them to the lot, where the police had found incriminating tissues. While this evidence was enough to make the lot a common bawdy house under the Criminal Code of Canada, it would not support a charge that the women were "keepers." Keepers could be trespassers, as the prostitutes were at the lot, but they must also at least attempt to have real control over the premises. Here, the prosecution had led no evidence that the women directed their customers to the lot, or that they had the slightest interest in which space the customer used, much less a rental agreement with the lot's owner.

Presented with the notion that a house could be a patch of undeveloped, cold, barren land, the mediaeval tenant would probably have taken to his bed, hiding under the covers and praying to God and the angels for a solid week. In a time when people conveyed land by dropping a clod at the feet of the buyer, even very businesslike (but metaphysical) conveniences such as *escrow*, householder *equity*, *land flips* (where a buyer owns land only on paper, and sometimes only for very short intervals, in order to make a quick profit speculating with it), not to say mortgages might well have been characterized as hallucinations caused by demonic possession. Yet, in an age when outdoor heating vents are all the home growing numbers of poor people know, it is probably not so extraordinary that a parking lot should be a bawdy house. In the 1980s, when the landed really are in a sense "gentry," "You've come a long way baby!" has taken on a sardonic, even bitter, cast.

CHAPTER SIX

Rubes and Slickers

This contract is so one-sided that I am astonished to find it written
on both sides of the paper.

Attributed to Lord Evershed

A learned County Court judge in a book of memoirs recently said
that an overwhelming amount of his time on the bench was taken
up "with people who are persuaded by persons whom they do not
know to enter into contracts that they do not understand to purchase goods that they do not want with money that they have not
got."

Lord Greene, Master of the Rolls, 1944

In his little moral tale, "Political Economy," Mark Twain purports
to be in the midst of writing a very highbrow essay on economics when
a lightning-rod salesman knocks at his door. Distracted, anxious to
get back to his work before all inspiration is drummed out, Twain
tells the man to do as he likes with the house so long as he doesn't
disturb the closeted writer. Eventually, the lesson on political economy

comes not from Twain's essay but from what happens when an electrical storm hits the county, turning Twain's retrofitted house into a fireworks extravaganza that inspires him to enter a new agreement with local handymen to reduce the number of rods from "a stack of them" to four.

The scenario is typical of what in the 1960s and seventies were called "high-pressure sales." When presented with the final bill, Twain might say he agreed to the first transactions under duress (in the colloquial sense; as a legal "term of art," duress usually means pressure exerted with violence or threats of violence, as in the Egyptian marriage contract case in Chapter Two) or in an altered state of consciousness, which itself caused more duress that forced him into the new contract for a reduced number of rods. He might even plead mental incompetence.

But is it reasonable to impede the necessary business of the world — the genuine "political economy" — by calling common problems of everyday living "duress" or "undue pressure"? Should we excuse buyers from their obligations just because they were distracted, missed their squash game or therapy appointment, were "stressed out" during negotiations? Can the salesman be said to have exerted extraordinary pressure on Twain just by showing up when he did? Did he really misrepresent anything?

Obviously, there was consideration flowing both ways: Twain got lightning rods, the salesman got paid. And there seem to have been a valid offer and acceptance. The salesman told Twain exactly what he was getting, and Twain agreed. Bizarrely, had Twain actually gone out to a hardware store determined to buy lightning rods, the common law would have required much more deliberate action of him to make the contract good.

You would think that by displaying lightning rods at thirty cents a foot, your hardware store is offering to sell them, and that by taking a rod to the cashier you are accepting that offer. But the common law says that the store is inviting *you* to make an offer by picking up a rod and taking it to the cashier — "I'll buy your lightning rod for thirty cents a foot" — which the store can accept or refuse. When you go to the store, you are the offeror — you are offering to *purchase*, even though the seller has set the price. (Presumably, but unrealistically, it is open to you as offeror to barter the price down.) One "justification" for this rule, nonetheless ridiculous because endorsed by judges, is that, once you accept an offer, you cannot rescind the deal. If taking a Zeus lightning rod into your hands at a self-serve store constituted "acceptance," you could not change your mind, set the Zeus rod down and choose a Thor lightning rod instead. Such reasoning of course ignores the fact that you wouldn't really accept an offer in a self-serve store until you were ready to pay for your selection.

The fact that the rule was formulated in a case about the sale of nonprescription drugs, ones containing minute quantities of codeine and strychnine, makes it somewhat less eccentric: the idea that the pharmacist could decide whether to accept a self-serve customer's "offer" allowed him to control who bought potentially dangerous drugs and for what purpose. Before legislatures stepped in, this arrangement meant that, technically, a cashier, the offeree, could make a counteroffer and change the price just when you were ready to buy an item for the price marked. As well, it allowed "bait and switch": because stores were not offering anything, *per se*, they could display merchandise they were not selling to lure customers in to buy other, less attractive, goods.

(It is also notable that the rule was invented in Britain, where custom has forbidden patrons at a vegetable stand, for example, to choose their own produce from the goods "on offer." The vendor selects the produce, clearly offering to sell it.)

The situation becomes even more bemusing when the offer is said to be contained in advertising. Suppose Twain saw an ad in the *Calaveras Picayune* that said Zeus lightning rods boasted a special manufacturer's guarantee. Zeus, the ad touted, had even set up a trust fund for anyone purchasing the rods whose house was hit and damaged by lightning. Twain buys a Zeus rod at his hardware store and it doesn't work. He writes Zeus to make a claim from the trust fund, enclosing photos of the fire and water damage to his roof, soffits, and masonry. Zeus refuses to pay, saying Twain never informed them of his purchase when he made it, so he never accepted their offer to insure him against lightning damage.

Substitute a "carbolic smokeball" for lightning rods, and you have a leading case in the common law of offer and acceptance, *Carlill v. Carbolic Smoke Ball Company*. The plaintiff, Mrs. Carlill, based her suit on an ad published in 1891, in which the defendant company promised to pay a one-hundred-pound reward to anyone who used their "refillable" product for two weeks, three times a day, and still caught "influenza, colds, or any disease caused by taking cold." "During the last epidemic of influenza," the ad said, "many thousand carbolic smoke balls were sold as preventives against this disease, and in no ascertained case was the disease contracted by those using the carbolic smoke ball." The company also claimed to have deposited one thousand pounds with the Alliance Bank "shewing our sincerity in the matter."

Mrs. Carlill had used the smoke ball according to directions for nearly two months, yet had still come down with the flu. She wrote to Carbolic, and after they refused her claim she pursued it before the courts, hiring the son of novelist Charles Dickens to act as her leading counsel. When she won at trial and Carbolic appealed, Lord Justice Nathaniel Lindley dismissed Carbolic's contention that the ad was nothing more than a bet with the customer that she wouldn't get the flu — a nervy tactic by the company, but creative insofar as illegal bets are unenforceable in courts of law. Neither was the advertising mere "puffery," the court held, the sort of hype that no one took as a promise: the business about the thousand-pound deposit "shewing our sincerity" put the lie to that. The offer to pay a hundred pounds was a "promise, as plain as words can make it."

Carbolic bounced back with the assertion that the ad couldn't be a legally binding offer because it wasn't made to anyone in particular. It was just floating around out there. Justice Lindley agreed that the offer was free-floating, but added that, as in the rewards cases like *Williams v. Carwardine*, the ad was a perfectly legal *continuing* offer to the world at large — an offer accepted whenever anybody performed its terms; or, if it could be said that the contract was complete only when someone notified Carbolic that she had accepted the offer, Carbolic was duly notified of acceptance whenever anyone wrote to claim the hundred-pound "reward."

Pulling out all the stops, Carbolic ventured that the deal was invalid because there was no consideration. It was a naked promise because there was nothing in it for them. What if someone had stolen one of the balls, they asked, and claimed the reward? There would be no consideration passing to them from the thief, no benefit to the company. Never mind rogues and thieves, Justice Lindley replied. Consideration would pass if, on the strength of the ad's promise, alone, Carbolic could "only get the public to have confidence enough" to use the smoke ball. Besides, anyone who took the product seriously enough to use it according to the directions put herself "to some inconvenience at the request of the defendants" — gave consideration in the form of her effort and time. If Carbolic had "been so unwary as to expose themselves to a great many actions, so much the worse for them."

More subtle promotion may be fraught with just as many pitfalls. If you want to advertise your business in the phone book, for instance, you are dealing with a public utility, a creature of statute. Statute law may give the utility a power even greater than the retailer's common-law influence over your freedom to contract.

Say, for example, you are in the business of hauling trash ardently; for all appearances you are determined to be *the* premier trash hauler in Tulsa, if not Oklahoma and beyond. In the white pages, you can be found under A ash cans, A Aaa Accurate Trash Clean-up, A Aaab Trash Service, AAbbreviated Credit Trash Service, A Aaactable Trash Hauling Service, A Aaabandon-All Trash Service . . . — thus implying that beyond being simply top of the heap (the competition being somehow "inaccurate" about hauling garbage) as well as feverishly industrious to the tune of spelling "actable" with three a's, you might even offer the milk of human kindness with easy credit terms. If there is any doubt, customers can find you in the yellow pages under Ash Cans, Hauling; Trash Burners; Trash Hauling; and Trash Incineration, heading the list in each category as Ace, AAAA, AAAb Trash Service, AAbandon-All. . . .

In the 1960s, these tactics were employed by a genuine waste-disposal company managed by Robert and Fern Williams, proprietors of what they at last registered with the Oklahoma Corporation Commission as AAAAAAAAAAAAAAAAAAAAAA Inc. Evidently they wanted to secure their preeminence absolutely. But when they tried to contract with Southwestern Bell in 1961 to list them in the phone books under that insuperable name, Southwestern refused.

Clearly not the sort of people to take no, or even "that's enough," for an answer, Robert and Fern asked the Corporation Commission to intervene. When the commission refused to order Southwestern to list the name, Robert and Fern appealed to the Oklahoma Supreme Court. All eight judges sitting on the case agreed that giving the Williamses' trash-hauling business such grandiose alphabetical superiority would be unfair to their competition. Otherwise, the judges said, every business would soon be trying to out-A and outlist competing businesses, until "finally a mockery of the telephone directory system would result." You would need, the court implied, a dump truck to carry the phone book around.

It based its decision in part on another 8:0 holding, one from 1924 concerning Fred Harvey, a food service connected with the railways when eating railway food had a *je ne sais quoi* that had nothing to do with artificial ingredients and flash freezing. Harvey had appealed an order of the Corporation Commission chairman forcing them to seat men not wearing jackets in their dining rooms; their preferred practice had been to ask the shirtsleeved to pay a la carte prices at a lunch counter. Noting that Harvey provided jackets to patrons not wearing them, the court found that "unlike lower animals, we all demand the maintenance of some style and fashion in the dining room," and accepted the evidence of two anthropologists that such social conventions promoted decorum, societal harmony and "a wholesome psychological effect."

Judge J.D. Lydick, writing for the court, castigated the corporation commission for trying to run the railways: "Lawmakers," he cried from his high horse, "must not completely destroy personal liberty" — meaning, evidently, that the commission should not be telling Harvey whom it could deal with, on what terms. He even marshalled the incumbent U.S. president to Harvey's side, quoting Calvin Coolidge's remark that "a citizen of a real republic cannot exist as a segregated, unattached fragment of selfishness" — all of us must occasionally bow to convention. As often happens when "freedom of contract" is the focus of a dispute, the court seemed to forget that there were two sides to such freedom — that the ordinary shirtsleeved Joe, out for a good, inexpensive feed, is a free citizen, too, in need of considerably more state protection than public conglomerates would be. Judge Lydick glosses over the subtler anthropology — that a man might eschew dress-jackets because he can't accommodate them financially or, if he really likes his feed, physically, at least not without discomfort or embarrassment, especially if he is crammed into "a loaner." Then, again, maybe he is a fashion pioneer, plumping for the casual look.

Conventional legal wisdom has always said that the typical contest for the promotion of consumer products — a draw, say, for a car or television set — amounts to an illegal lottery. In *United States v. One Box of Tobacco, "Footprints,"* it was held that packing coupons in boxes of tobacco, tiny tin footprints redeemable at fifty cents apiece, could amount to an illegal lottery. The *Criminal Code of Canada* makes it an indictable offense — a felony — to hold an unauthorized lottery or to profit from any game of chance. There are similar laws in many of the United States. In recent years, governments have been excused from these prescriptions, but of course cynics will say that governments have never needed permission to gamble away the people's bread and butter. In fact, in 1982, one such dissenter, a man named John Turmel, attempted to have the governor of the Bank of Canada indicted for running a common gaming house, as well as for genocide: the governor's interest policies, Turmel said, were "killing people." The Supreme Court of Canada did not agree. (More recently, Turmel stirred up politics again by running for all three levels of government in a single election.)

In 1965, the Supreme Court of Washington declared that a referral sales scheme was an illegal lottery. Under the scheme, purchasers of Lifetone integrated intercom and alarm systems were told they could earn back at least the purchase price if they provided Lifetone with a list of potential purchasers. They were promised a one-hundred-dollar commission for each referral that ended in a purchase, and two hundred dollars for every fifteen referrals Lifetone approached without making a sale.

Clyde and Shirley Leach of Yakima County had agreed to this scheme, and had provided Lifetone with about sixty referrals. At Lifetone's request, they sent a form letter advising each referral that a "friend" would be calling soon to tell them about "a fabulous program." Lifetone instructed the Leaches not to contact the referrals until a salesman had done so.

Such referral schemes were widespread in the sixties, a time when credit cards carried a stigma among the middle class. Common to the schemes was an arrangement with a finance company (still customary in retail automobile sales) to lend purchasers the money to buy the product at the schemes' center. Lifetone arranged for the Leaches to sign such a financing contract, under which they promised to pay the purchase price of the intercom-alarm system, plus all interest, taxes and financing charges, whether they received any commissions or not.

The manufacturing cost of the intercom-alarm systems was $225.32. Lifetone sold the unit for about $900, but with financing charges, the total price to the Leaches was $1,187.28. In other words, fully twelve of their referrals would have to buy systems before the Leaches earned back their investment.

The supreme court compared the referral plan to a chain-letter scheme, toting up the stupendous odds against 12 additional sales for every firm one. Once the first investor in the scheme bought a system, 12 of his referrals would have to buy; then 144 would have to buy from the next purchasers (12 for each of those 12), and then 1,728 (12 for each of those 144), and so on exponentially (as in the impossibility cases in Chapter Three!) — until by just the fifth round, half the people in the entire city of Seattle would have to buy the alarms for the initial purchasers to earn back their investments. In their book *The Dark Side of the Marketplace*, W.G. Magnuson and J. Carper extrapolate from this to conclude that by as early as the eighth round a population equivalent to that of all of Europe would have had to buy alarm systems, and by the ninth round there would not have been enough people on the entire planet for the scheme to work, even if every man, woman and child of them made a purchase.

The Lifetone scheme ran for six months. By the time the Leaches bought their system, it had been underway for five, and Lifetone had paid out $14,900 in commissions to sixty-five purchasers. The Leaches, snared in the quantum mathematics of late-round purchase, did not receive a single commisson. By the time the scheme ended, twenty-two other purchasers would find themselves in the same deflated state.

In their defense, Lifetone pointed to the $14,900 paid out, and insisted that the shifting winds of chance had very little to do with the scheme: both the referees and salesmen were obliged to exercise skill and judgment, they told the court, the referees in choosing those

they recommended as potential purchasers, and the salesmen in closing the deals. But the court held that the Leaches were taking all
sorts of gambles — on whether the referrals would be interested or
already referred by someone else, on whether the salesmen would do
a competent job — and had been pressed by Lifetone to surrender
any control over the sales by not contacting the referrals. The finance
company was not entitled to its money: it had full knowledge of the
illegal lottery Lifetone was running, and therefore its contract with
the Leaches, which sprang from the contract for the alarm system,
was illegal. Moreover, the Leaches' promise to pay the finance company notwithstanding the referral scheme was no contract at all.
Inasmuch as the alarm system had been installed and the commission scheme arranged before the finance company entered the picture, they were offering the Leaches no additional benefit — no consideration: a naked promise.

With *legal* lotteries run by the state, charities and other authorized
bodies, a whole raft of collateral problems has arisen. In 1985, for
instance, a Toronto woman won half of a $600,000 lottery prize in
court proceedings against a paramour, even though the man denied
that he'd ever been more than mildly friendly with the woman, let
alone her contractual partner in a gambling enterprise. (Although
the man paid for the ticket, the court held the woman's consideration to be "love and affection and picking the numbers.") What God
hath joined, lucre can instantly put asunder. Until an English court
intervened in a case thirty years earlier, an eighty-three-year-old
landlady refused to share the £750 she won from a newspaper competition in partnership with her lodger. She claimed, unsuccessfully,
that the lodger was only "helping" her fill in the contest form; that
she, the landlady, had paid the postage to send the winning form
to the newspaper; and that neither of them "intended legal consequences" when they worked together on the competition. (That is,
insofar as they were a sort of "family," any agreements they made
were too casual and intimate to be enforceable at law. The postage
would represent part of the consideration paid by a person entering
the contest — in return for a chance to win a prize — and if paying
it had not been shared week to week among the landlady, her grand-
daughter and the lodger, the landlady's claim that she paid it might

have added weight to her contention that the lodger was only "helping" her enter the contest.)

In addition to more frequent state prosecutions for lottery ticket forgeries and fraudulent prize claims, parent has been suing child these days, and neighbor contending with neighbor for a share of lottery stakes. When a ticket comes up lucky, it is not unusual for the holder to "forget" or repudiate agreements made to share the proceeds. As disclosed in *Quiamco v. Gaspar*, for example, the defendant owned a ten-dollar lottery ticket but was short of the pocket money he needed to buy a piece of pipe. Quiamco paid for the pipe in return for half the lottery ticket. When the ticket hit for a million dollars, Gaspar "forgot" about the barter. No doubt he will not have the same problem remembering how the court found that Quiamco was entitled to half the lottery takings.

In a Pennsylvania case, a man who had spent six thousand dollars on lottery tickets claimed that because he was a compulsive gambler, the tickets represented illegal contracts. The state lottery commission, he said, knew, or should have known, of this mental illness that rendered him incompetent to make legally enforceable bargains — such as the purchase of lottery tickets. The man demanded reimbursement of his investment in the tickets, but the suit was dropped before it reached trial.

In New York in 1984, a plaintiff went so far as to claim lottery proceeds through divine intervention. The holder of the ticket in this instance was Daysi Fernandez, a thirty-eight-year-old welfare mother (until her luck changed) of three. The ticket had been purchased for her by her neighbor, sixteen-year-old Christopher Pando, whom Daysi had approached in the hope that the saint he claimed as his personal guardian, "St. Eleggua," would choose a winning number. If she could orchestrate it, Daysi hoped to leave everything to faith and nothing to chance.

Hedging her bets on young Christopher's piety, Daysi had given him four dollars, agreeing to share any winnings half and half. But when one of the tickets Christopher bought hit for $2,877,203.30, Daysi reneged, and poor Christopher eventually found himself in the New York Supreme Court, alleging breach of contract. There, Judge Edward Greenfield ruled that on at least two grounds Daysi's refusal

to share was not legally justified. First, even though the lottery corporation would pay out the money over ten years, she could not rely
on legislation that required oral contracts to be performed within
one year. All she had to do was tell the lottery commission to send
half of everything to Christopher and the promise to share would be
immediately executed, *within* a year.

Second, Daysi could not now argue that as a minor Christopher
had purchased the lottery tickets illegally. (Quite apart from the fact
that children cannot gamble, broadly speaking, minors can make
contracts only for things necessary to their subsistence; of course, a
nice question arises as to whether a million dollar lottery prize is
necessary to one's subsistence if one lives in grinding poverty.) Under
the state lottery laws, minors could receive tickets and winnings as
gifts, so Christopher could share the ticket with Daysi, as her gift to
him. The judge was stretching a point here (especially inasmuch as
he went on to find the arrangement to be a contract, not a gift), and
as far as Daysi was concerned, it was probably just as well: if
Christopher's purchase of the tickets was illegal, it was *nudum pactum*, making Daysi's interest also invalid.

Daysi's third defense took Judge Greenfield's fancy. If Christopher's
part of the bargain was to act as an intermediary between this and
the supernatural worlds, to perform "nothing less than a miracle,"
how could he prove in court that he'd lived up to that promise? True,
Judge Greenfield observed, Roman law accepted testimony from gods
and oracles and gave credence to assertions based on dreams. True,
too, in mediaeval times our own common law admitted evidence of
supposed miracles, and as late as the eighteenth century testimony
of spells was accepted in the prosecution of witches for causing natural
disasters. The judge might have added that, as recently as 1925,
testimony of religious faith was marshalled against science in the
famous Scopes "monkey trial."

But in this more "pragmatic era," the judge found, "the chasm
between the temporal and spiritual world has become unbridgeable."
Secular law did not believe in miracles. Their performance, being
a matter of faith rather than concrete fact, could not be consideration for a contract. Therefore Christopher could not meet his burden
of proof. Without St. Eleggua in the flesh, he could not show "on

a balance of probabilities" that he had performed his end of the deal. Because the contract was invalid, Daysi was not obliged to share the lottery takings.

As for "St. Eleggua," Judge Greenfield had gone looking for him in Butler's *Lives of the Saints*, but could find there only St. Eligius, the "St. Elsewhere" of television, patron saint of goldsmiths "who showered his riches on the poor." It was no wonder, the judge added, that Daysi wanted such a saint's help. No wonder, indeed. According to the *Oxford Dictionary of Saints*, St. Eligius's emblem was a horseshoe. And his name, says the *Catholic Dictionary*, can be found on third-of-a-sou coins from the seventh century.

Then again, St. Eligius preached loud and long against magic, charms and supplications to the gods to intercede in human affairs. So the case was proved, if not in court, at least in the school of hard knocks. Perhaps St. Eligius had fabricated a golden object-lesson for young Christopher, one that he will not likely forget. "If you would know what the Lord God thinks of money," Maurice Baring once wrote, "you have only to look at those to whom he gives it" — Daysi Fernandez excepted, of course.

The Canadian *Criminal Code* does allow the populace to profit from "games of skill" if not from unregulated sport of pure chance. Before the law was changed to permit games of "mixed skill and chance" as well, the Supreme Court of Canada ruled that you could not make money at playing contract bridge, for instance, even though the only element of chance was in the dealing of the cards. At that time, the proportion of luck to skill in a game was deemed irrelevant.

But once the combination of skill and luck was legal, the "skill-testing question" became a prominent component of product promotion contests. You might "scratch-and-win" one hundred dollars on a coupon, but such a win was illegal unless you could answer a question or perform some act that supposedly taxed your acuity. On the rationale that most adults, regardless of language skills, upbringing, or education, will enjoy at least rudimentary mathematical abilities, the question is usually arithmetical, an option that has the added benefit of meeting the legal requirement that the "skill" be more than the performance of a ridiculously simple task. With seemingly profound injustice, peeling potatoes was ruled out in one case, while in another, it was deemed legal to require contestants to estimate the time it would take barrels to travel between two points on a river.

But even with numbers, lawful "skill testing" may itself be an utter gamble. The events leading to *Ranger v. Herbert A. Watts Ltd.*, for example, might have come off "The Honeymooners" or "I Love Lucy." In fact, the presiding judge, Justice Edson Haines of the High Court of Ontario, wrote in his decision that its evidence "assumes the character of a television comedy and reminds one that truth can be stranger than fiction."

In 1968, Ernest Ranger, a trucker, had opened a carton of Peter Jackson cigarettes, his regular brand, to find a certificate for a ten-thousand-dollar "cash award." As Ranger had broken his reading glasses, his wife read the fine print to him: Ranger was to contact Peter Jackson's agent, Herbert A. Watts Limited, giving his name, other personal information and the serial number on the certificate. To win, he would be asked to answer a "time-limited skill-testing question." Mrs. Ranger mailed the required information to Watts and awaited developments.

While the Rangers waited, their friends played jokes on them, phoning up and pretending to be the cigarette people. But by the end of February, Ernest Ranger wasn't in much of a humor. That week, one of his employees had rolled his dump truck. Because the accident was not the result of a collision, it was not covered by insurance. It would cost three thousand dollars to repair, not to mention the income lost to Ranger while it was out of service. Ranger estimated his annual income at the time at only four thousand dollars.

The Rangers were also in the process of redecorating their living room, and when the phone rang in there on the evening of Friday, March 1, 1968, Ernest's daughter had to answer it by squatting where the phone sat on the floor near the television set. The television gave off the only light in the room, unless you figured in the haze that filtered down the hall from the kitchen. Ernest had spent the day welding the damage to his truck, and when the phone rang he had been lying in bed trying to fend off a headache and rest his tired eyes. He still was without his reading glasses. His daughter came into his bedroom to tell him Mrs. Haas, the wife of one of his employees, was calling.

When Ranger picked up the phone, the woman on the other end

said she was Jeanne Emelyanov of Herbert A. Watts Limited, and asked him if he could spare "about five minutes." Young Ms. Ranger had evidently misjudged the voice. When Ranger agreed to talk to Emelyanov, unsure whether this was another joke, she asked him to verify his cash award serial number.

"Just a moment, please," Ranger said. He hurried to get his wife, who was talking to her mother on another phone in the kitchen. Ranger must have said something like, "It's the cigarette people about the money!" for, suddenly, the whole family — Ranger, his wife, their three teenage children — and two neighborhood girlfriends of the children, were gathered around the television in the gloaming of the unfinished living room.

Emelyanov began reciting the math question to Ranger, who had nothing to write on and couldn't see to write, anyway. The rest of the family scrabbled to find pencil and paper, and fought over what they did find, as Ranger yelled out the numbers and operations to his wife. Unfortunately, on top of everything else, Mrs. Ranger was nearly deaf, and the family had been too strapped to afford complete treatment for her hearing problems. When Emelyanov asked Ranger to read the question back to her before she began timing him, he would at first try to read the scribbled-up paper his wife thrust at him in the dark, then give up and try to recall the question from memory. The conversation between Emelyanov and Ranger is recorded in the case report as follows:

Judge: Mr. Ranger?
Answer: Yes.
Judge: Are you Mr. Ernest Lorenzo Ranger?
Ranger: Right.
Judge: Did you find a Peter Jackson Cash Award Certificate?
Ranger: (Indecipherable) — Speaking.
Judge: Good evening, sir. This is Jeanne Emelyanov calling. I am representing the panel of judges for the manufacturers of Peter Jackson cigarettes. Now, is it convenient for you to give us about 5 minutes of your time on the phone at this time?
Ranger: Yes.
Judge: All right. Thank you. Now, first of all, would you please confirm the serial number appearing on your Certificate?

Ranger: Just a moment please.

Judge: Thank you.

(Pause)

Ranger: Hello.

Judge: Yes.

Ranger: TR 5010.

Judge: 5010. Fine. Now as the rules clearly stated, Mr. Ranger, this promotion is open to persons 18 years of age or older. Therefore would you mind confirming your age.

Ranger: 45.

Judge: Thank you. Now for our reference we are saying that today is Friday, March 1st, 1968 and it is now ten minutes to six.

Ranger: Yes.

Judge: I would ask you to bear with me if you hear any noise on the telephone connection. The beep signal which you hear periodically indicates that we are taperecording our conversation, so I would ask you to kindly speak clearly and loudly so we can pick it up entirely.

Ranger: Yes. Okay.

Judge: Now, are you or any member of your immediate family employed by the manufacturers of Peter Jackson cigarettes?

Ranger: No.

Judge: By their affiliates, their agents, their advertising agencies or by Herbert A. Watts (Quebec) Limited?

Ranger: No.

Judge: Thank you. Are you employed, Mr. Ranger?

Ranger: Well, self-employed. I'm a truck driver.

Judge: You are self-employed — self-employed. All right. And, where do you usually buy your Peter Jackson cigarettes, Mr. Ranger?

Ranger: Oh, well, anywhere handy. I usually buy them by the carton.

Judge: And you usually buy them by the carton. Fine. Thank you very much. Now in order to conform to the published rules of this promotion, you are now required to correctly answer this skill-testing question. Do you have a pencil and paper handy?

Ranger: Yes.

Judge: All right. The question is a mathematical one, Mr. Ranger . . .

Ranger: Just a moment please.

(Pause)

Ranger: Yes.

Judge: Yes. The question is a mathematical one, as I was saying. We will read it to you slowly, then to be sure you have taken it down correctly we will ask you to repeat it to us. After that you will have one and a half minutes from the time we say so to calculate the answer. Is that clear?

Ranger: Yes.

Judge: All right. Are you ready to take down the question?

Ranger: Yes.

Judge: Here it is. Multiply . . .

Ranger: Multiply . . .

Judge: Twenty-four by six.

Ranger: Twenty-four by six.

Judge: Add . . .

Ranger: Add . . .

Judge: Three hundred and eighty-eight.

Ranger: Three hundred and eighty-eight.

Judge: Divide by seven.

Ranger: Divide by seven.

Judge: And finally subtract thirty-eight.

Ranger: And finally subtract thirty-eight.

Judge: Right. Now would you repeat that to me before you start, please.

Ranger: (No comment)

Judge: Mr. Ranger, will you repeat the question to me before you start working on it please?

Ranger: (Pause) It's . . . (Pause) I didn't write it down.

Judge: Would you repeat the question to me, Mr. Ranger?

Ranger: (more loudly) I didn't write them down, as a—

Judge: Well, how did you expect to work it out . . .

Ranger: (No comment)

Judge: Hello . . . Mr. Ranger . . .

Ranger: Yes.

Judge: Would you repeat that question to me. You . . . You
Ranger: Oh . . . I put the twenty-four . . .
Judge: Well, I'll repeat it to you now, would you copy it down
        please.
Ranger: Yes.
Judge: Multiply twenty-four by six.
Ranger: Multiply twenty-four by six.
Judge: Add three hundred and eighty-eight.
Ranger: Add three hundred and eighty-eight.
Judge: Divide by seven.
Ranger: Divide by seven.
Judge: Subtract thirty-eight.
Ranger: And subtract thirty-eight.
Judge: Now will you repeat it to me please.
Ranger: Yes. Add twenty . . .
        (Pause)
Judge: Mr. Ranger, we'll have to disqualify you if you don't read
        this back to us immediately.
Ranger: Yes . . . Add twenty-four . . .
Judge: No, it's multiply . . .
Ranger: Multiply twenty-four . . .
Judge: By six.
Ranger: By six.
Judge: Right.
Ranger: Add three eighty-eight.
Judge: Right.
Ranger: Subtract thirty-seven.
Judge: No. Divide by seven.
Ranger: Divide by seven.
Judge: Divide by seven, and subtract . . .
Ranger: Subtract thirty-eight.
Judge: Have you got it straight now?
Ranger: Yes.
Judge: Or do you want to read it back?
Ranger: No, I think I have it.
Judge: Would you read it again, please, Mr. Ranger?
Ranger: (Pause)
        Add twenty-four by six.
Judge: Multiply.

Ranger: Multiply.
Ranger: Add three eighty-eight.
Judge: Yes.
Ranger: Subtract . . .
Judge: No, divide . . .
Ranger: Divide by seven.
Judge: Right.
Ranger: And a . . . add thirty-eight.
Judge: Subtract.
Ranger: Subtract thirty-eight rather.
Judge: Have you got it straight now, Mr. Ranger?
Ranger: Yes.
Judge: All right, you have one and a half minutes. Go ahead, please.
　　　　(Pause — 75 seconds)
Judge: Fifteen seconds left.
　　　　(Pause — 15 seconds)
Judge: All right, Mr. Ranger, your time is up. May I have your answer?
Ranger: A hundred and fourteen.
Judge: I beg your pardon?
Ranger: A hundred and fourteen.
Judge: No, I'm sorry, sir. A hundred and fourteen is not the right answer. I am very sorry. Thank you very much and good night sir.

Justice Haines went out of his way to find that, at law, this exchange did not amount to a skill-testing question. It was unfair, he found, because there was no "reasonable advance notice," no "communication beforehand of the rules by which the test will be conducted" and no attempt by the examiner to determine whether the contestant was "in a reasonable condition to engage in the test." While there was no precedent for such criteria, and even though Ranger had told Emelyanov it was "convenient" for him to talk, the judgment stood on appeal. Today, many contest promotions in Canada include the advisory, "In order to win, the selected entrant(s) must first correctly answer a time-limited mathematical skill-testing question to be administered by telephone at a pre-arranged, mutually convenient time."

The evidence of a school mathematics expert who testified at the *Ranger* trial makes an interesting sidelight on the case: according to "the universal rules of mathematics," the expert said, the answer to the problem read by Emelyanov is not 38, as Emelyanov and Watts believed it to be, but 161.43: $(24 \times 6) + (388 \div 7) - 8$; *not* 24×6, then add 388, then divide by 7, etc. In one of the exhibits entered at the trial, it is clear that Ranger's son arrived at the mathematician's answer — $161^3/_7$.

The Lifetone alarms case is of course idiosyncratic among court decisions on retail contracts. If such a sale offends, it is usually not because it works as an "illegal lottery," but because it involves unfair or "unconscionable" business practices such as "fraudulent misrepresentation." The seller is not excused if the buyer is unusually susceptible to manipulation; indeed, this works against the seller inasmuch as the courts often assume that weaker consumers are the unethical salesman's chief prey.

A 1969 Canadian case, for example, tells of a vacuum-cleaner salesman who showed up at the door of a "decent, simple" couple with no regular income. He told the woman of the house that he had a surprise for her, to which she replied that she had just purchased a vacuum cleaner and her husband was out of work. The salesman assured her he wasn't selling vacuum cleaners but wanted to show her a book about all the wonderful labor-saving devices manufactured by his company.

The woman allowed the salesman into her house, where he showed the book to her, her husband and her son, and then told them he had a surprise for them in the car, courtesy of this wonder-working manufacturer who employed him. Upon being cautioned not to bother bringing the surprise in if it was a vacuum cleaner, the salesman retrieved a box from his car and asked the family to guess what was inside it. The son thought it was a vacuum cleaner. Over the family's protests, the salesman insisted on demonstrating it. In disgust, the father and son fled to the basement.

After the demonstration, the salesman explained to the woman how she could make money while her husband was out of work by sending letters (like those in the Lifetone case) to her friends and relatives relating that she had "arranged" for them to see the demonstration. All she had to do was copy, thirty times, in her own handwriting, a formula pitch admitting to her correspondents that they were no doubt "surprised" to hear from her, but "John and I have recently been given the opportunity to see a most interesting exhibition plus a pleasant surprise and a chance to earn some extra money." She was to add that the referrals were under no obligation, and that "knowing you as we do, you will be as impressed as we were."

While "impressed" might not have been the word the woman would have chosen herself, the salesman assured her that each time one of her referrals bought a vacuum cleaner, his company would pay her $25. With nine such sales (totalling $225), the cleaner he had just demonstrated would be hers to keep, "free of charge." He convinced the woman to pay a deposit and sign both a conditional sales agreement and a promissory note, then followed her to the basement to secure her sequestered husband's signature as well. As the salesman prepared to leave, the family asked him to take the vacuum cleaner back to the car, but he refused, saying the cleaner could not be resold because it was "used."

The family later received one $25 check from the vacuum cleaner company. They did not cash it, nor did they open the box with the new vacuum cleaner in it. Nor did they pay on the promissory note when the company demanded $252.72 plus costs and lawyer's fees amounting to, yes, $25. Based on the evidence that the salesman had claimed not to be selling a vacuum cleaner but "giving the defendants an opportunity to earn money and receive a free vacuum cleaner as a bonus," Judge Leach of the Ontario County Court had no trouble finding fraudulent misrepresentation, excusing the family from their obligation to pay once they had returned the vacuum cleaner.

Outside vacuum cleaner referral cases (and allied ones such as the Lifetone case, or those having to do with the sale of aluminum siding), the most notorious retail fraud actions, and certainly the most poignant ones, are lawsuits stemming from dance-studio contracts.

Door-to-door vacuum cleaner sales have been a casualty of the two-income family; if anyone is home to answer the knock, it will be the babysitter, who does the housework but has no say in purchasing the necessary equipment. But loneliness remains a given in the human condition, and there seems always to be someone poised to make a dollar on the impetuous behavior it can inspire. Typically, in the dance-studio scenarios, a lonely, shy young woman will sign up for lessons in the hope of meeting men in a "safe" environment. The dance studio will cater to this weakness, often assigning their most charming and persuasive instructor to the lonelyheart, to flatter and excite her into signing up for thousands of dollars worth of lessons. Likely some of the "students" see through the ruse, but are willfully blind. They are reasonably happy with the arrangement, and often go deeply into debt, until it becomes clear that nothing much is in the offing beyond learning very much more about the fox trot and rumba than they really want to know. As one judge put in a particularly cruel instance, "Thankfully, during the signing of the later contracts one of the clauses was deleted. It was a clause to the effect that all of the lessons had to be used up within a year. This poor lady would have been dancing night and day if that clause had not been deleted."

The "poor lady" was a thirty-one-year-old nurse who had committed herself to more than $6,500 worth of dance lessons — 222 hours privately, 347 hours in a group — with a British Columbia outfit called Fiesta Dance Studios. (With supreme *chutzpah*, it sometimes also styled itself "Fred Astaire Dance Studios.") She had also signed up for lessons with a teacher who had left Fiesta. When she eventually tried to rescind the Fiesta contracts, complaining of a bad knee and that the instruction ws not meeting her expectations, the British Columbia Supreme Court permitted her to rescind only one, related to something Fiesta called the "Gold Key Club."

The woman's instructor had told her that it was the highest honor for a student to be asked to join this club and that, because of her great dancing ability and other charms, he was prepared to put her name forward for prospective membership. She would be asked to audition, he said, and if she succeeded, she would become an honorary staff member enjoying certain staff perks, including the privilege of socializing with the instructors.

Flattered and flustered, the woman accepted the invitation, after which she was made to dance before a "three-member board" and a camera. The final decision, the instructor said, would be reached once the film was screened by head office in New York. When the audition ended, a cheer went up among the instructors. Cake was sliced, champagne poured and a contract proffered for $2,573 — putatively to bring the woman "up to the standards required of a

Gold Key member." In the flush of the moment she giddily signed. No one told her that the camera had no film in it and that the audition was "a standing joke among the staff members."

Justice H.C. McKay found that the staff was reasonably qualified to teach dancing, and that the woman had entered all the contracts but the Gold Key one "with her eyes open." But the Gold Key affair "was a demeaning, cruel and fraudulent hoax." Out of the nearly $7,000 she owed, the woman was excused $2,573 plus legal costs.

In an earlier case, another nurse, a twenty-four-year-old German immigrant, had committed herself to contracts totaling $1,047.50. Although her annual income was only $1,800, the Manitoba Court of Appeal held her to her agreements. "It is not the function of the Courts," one judge wrote, "to protect adults from improvident bargains. That this was a ridiculous bargain is beyond doubt, but if the case did not go beyond that plaintiff [the nurse] could not succeed." The nurse had become enamored of her glib instructor, but the tactics of the studio had not descended to the level of the "Gold Key" hoax in the *Fiesta* case.

"Little guy" or consumer-oriented law reached a dramatic apex in 1974 with a case called *Lloyds Bank v. Bundy*. Before then, if there had not been fraud or misrepresentation by a party to a contract, it was still possible to avoid a contract if it was made under duress or similar unfairness. But there was no clear and comprehensive statement of what after *Bundy* has been dubbed "the doctrine of unconscionability."

The judgment of Lord Denning in the case is so sympathetic and compelling, its opening words have become famous:

> Broadchalke is one of the most pleasing villages in England. Old Herbert Bundy, the defendant, was a farmer there. His home was at Yew Tree Farm. It went back for 300 years. His family had been there for generations. It was his only asset. But he did a very foolish thing. He mortgaged it to the bank. Up to the very hilt.

In fact, Bundy had mortgaged Yew Tree Farm away by dribs and drabs during three years, each time in an attempt to prop up his son's business failures. Even though his solicitor had advised him not to pledge more than half the farm's value of £10,000, Bundy mortgaged it to Lloyds to secure £7,500. When the son's finances worsened and the bank threatened to bankrupt him, Bundy pledged the entire farm to hold the bank off. By this time, a new manager was handling the account, and he did not suggest to Bundy that he get independent legal advice. On the other hand, Bundy's wife was present at the signing of the mortgage papers, as were his son and daughter-in-law.

Although Bundy was "a poor old gentleman" who owned nothing but Yew Tree — and who suffered a heart attack in the witness box while narrating the sad tale of his dealings with Lloyds — the trial judge ruled that the bank had the clear right to seize the farm and sell it. But on appeal, Lord Denning found that there had been such "inequality of bargaining power" between Bundy and Lloyds that the second mortgage was no good. To reach this conclusion, his lordship consolidated all the cases that could be grouped under the "inequality" rubric — contracts made when someone held property to pressure a person to bargain; agreements to the overwhelming advantage of a person of privilege, special power or higher knowledge and ability; agreements made under the pressure of overwhelming affection or need; and salvage agreements made during the panic of ships in distress. And he held that the gist of these cases was that the law

> gives relief to one who, without independent advice, enters into a contract upon terms which are very unfair or transfers property for a consideration which is grossly inadequate, when his bargaining power is grievously impaired by reason of his own needs or desires, or by his own ignorance or infirmity, coupled with undue influences or pressures brought to bear on him by or for the benefit of the other.

Bundy, "impaired" by fatherly feeling, had placed his faith in the bank manager, who unwittingly placed himself in a conflict of interest by acting as both banker and Bundy's adviser. The bank manager should have advised Bundy to seek an expert opinion on the mortgage. There was no true "meeting of the minds" (a defense Mark Twain might like to have tried with the lightning-rod man). Beyond that, insofar as the son had already reached his credit limit of £10,000 before the second mortgage was signed, the bank had not given any new consideration for that mortgage. "All that the [son's] company gained was a short respite from impending doom."

Typically for Lord Denning and typically in this branch of the law, a judge strains to meet a hardship case. Generally, the law is not so forgiving when feeling blinds us or leads us to take foolish risks. "Unconscionability" is a very trendy notion, especially for the law of contracts. The banks would soon be out of the consumer loans business (and there would be many fewer debt-financed sports cars on the road, you would think) if they could enforce only those made after sober second thought and consultation with experts. The conventional legal view is crystallized in that famous 1875 dictum by another Master of the Rolls, Sir George Jessel, the view under which

> men of full age and competent understanding shall have the utmost liberty of contracting, and . . . their contracts when entered into freely and voluntarily shall be held sacred and shall be enforced by Courts of justice. Therefore, you have this paramount public policy to consider — that you are not lightly to interfere with this freedom of contract.

Short of fraud or misrepresentation, the conservative view, and the one that keeps the economy bubbling in North America, is the one familiar since the Norman Conquest and enunciated in the Manitoba dance case: a foolish bargain is a bargain all the same.

CHAPTER SEVEN

Authors and Readers,
Singers and Dancers

Twenty-five years ago, a typical essay on J.D. Salinger described the author's famous hermitage as "a unique accomplishment in American life," "a great joke on our time," a solitary protest against the cult of personality. Salinger's behavior has only strengthened his cult status. At sixty-eight, he remains probably the most famous unknown man of modern times.

His immense literary reputation rests on a single much-banned novel and a handful of stories. His last book appeared in 1963, and in 1965 he published a long story in the *New Yorker*. Since then, all that has been heard from him is a signature on a petition — Salinger being one of 154 protesting the dismissal of William Shawn as editor of the *New Yorker* — and a statement of claim filed in U.S. courts. But to publishers, and especially to critics and biographers, it is no joke that *Jerome David Salinger, A/K/A J.D. Salinger v. Random House Inc. and Ian Hamilton* may be the author's most consequential gift to posterity.

In July 1983, Salinger received a letter from Hamilton, a literary critic for the London *Sunday Times* who had just finished a biography of the poet Robert Lowell. Hamilton wrote that he had signed a deal for a similar project focusing on the mysterious author of *The Catcher in the Rye*. In fact, Random House had advanced Hamilton $100,000 for the book on Salinger, with the proviso that it must recount "something new." William Heinemann had purchased the British rights for £25,000.

One of the things J.D. Salinger has discovered since that summer day is that his carefully crafted isolation had already been violated by his own hand. But oblivious at the time, he wrote to Hamilton, "I think I have borne all the exploitation and loss of privacy I can possibly bear in a single lifetime." Yet, as researchers go, Hamilton can be a dogged one, and with at least $150,000 at stake, dogged is probably not a bad thing to be on a literary critic's salary. He pushed on, interviewing Salinger's agent, editors, publishers, old army buddies, school chums (he was a military school boy, like Holden Caulfield, the adolescent hero-narrator of *Catcher*), and neighbors in Cornish, New Hampshire, the town to which college students made Salinger-pilgrimages in the 1960s that themselves ran literally into a brick wall.

Hamilton had better fortune. He eventually dug up letters Salinger didn't know had been preserved — letters, for instance, from Salinger to his neighbor in Cornish, Learned Hand, once chief judge of the court which was about to play an intense role in the lives of both Salinger and Hamilton, as well as in the development of copyright law. After his death in 1961, Judge Hand's papers had been deposited at Harvard Law School. Letters from Salinger to his friends Elizabeth Murray and Whit Burnett (editor of *Story* magazine, where Salinger published early in his writing career) had been donated to the University of Texas and to Princeton.

Hamilton signed contracts at each university, agreeing not to reproduce the Salinger letters, or, in some cases, excerpts, without Salinger's permission. He finished *Salinger: A Writing Life* in the spring of 1986, and Random House began sending around galley proofs for prepublication review. *Publishers' Weekly* remarked that "in octogenarian judge Learned Hand, the solitary short story writer found a literary confessor," but found Hamilton's book sketchy.

Book List was a little more provocative. Their reviewer, Joanne Wilkinson, said that Hamilton portrayed his subject as arrogant "and constantly embroiled in arguments with his publishers." Hamilton pinned Salinger's hermitage on an "obsession" with his characters: he had begun "to think of them as if they were his real children . . . who must be sheltered from the hurtful scrutiny of critics." Still, Wilkinson found Hamilton's amateur psychologizing "a bit hard to take."

So, evidently, did J.D. Salinger, whose agent, Dorothy Olding, had tracked down a copy of the galleys. After reading them, Salinger instructed his lawyers at New York's Kaye Collyer and Boose to register the copyright in the seventy-nine letters Hamilton consulted, and to demand that Hamilton and Random House delete anything in the book derived from the letters.

Hamilton rewrote the book, paraphrasing most of the material he had excerpted from the letters, but Salinger persisted in his claims of piracy and filed suit. Yet on November 5, 1986, Judge Pierre Leval of the U.S. District Court ruled that Hamilton's use of the correspondence had been to "add color and accuracy of detail . . . [and] did not give the reader the sense that she has read Salinger's letters. The excerpting of these details does not interfere with Salinger's control over initial publication." Hamilton may have infringed Salinger's copyright, Judge Leval said, but the infringement was so limited as to fall within the legal exemptions called "fair use." Thus, neither had he breached his contracts with the universities, not to use the material without permission.

On December 3, Salinger's lawyers appeared before the U.S. Court of Appeals, where Judge Jon O. Newman reversed the District Court decision and ordered Random House not to distribute Hamilton's book until both sides presented their arguments at a full trial. Judge Newman admitted that "fair use" may be made of unpublished material, especially if serious scholars were the users; but, unlike Judge Leval, he felt bound by Gerald Ford's 1985 U.S. Supreme Court victory against the *Nation* magazine.

In the case, the magazine had "scooped" publishers Harper and Row, *Time* magazine and *Reader's Digest* by quoting and paraphrasing controversial letters from the ex-president's autobiography; Harper owned the rights to the hardcover book, *Time* and *Reader's Digest* had purchased excerpt rights. In finding for Gerald Ford, the Supreme Court "underscored the idea that unpublished letters normally enjoy insulation from fair use copying" — that is, they enjoy more protection than published letters do, or at least, with unpublished works, "fair" is more narrowly defined. In copyright law, "unpublished" is tantamount to "more private."

But Judge Newman entertained "the most serious disagreement" with Judge Leval on how much "infringing" material remained in Hamilton's revision of *Salinger: A Writing Life*. Hamilton could not avoid liability, Judge Newman said, simply by changing quotation to close paraphrase. If a Salinger war-time letter described a dog who "rides on the running board pointing out Nazis for me to arrest," it was not enough for Hamilton to change this to "rides with them in the car and lets them know if he spots any arrestable Nazis." And if another letter described U.S. politician Wendell Wilkie as looking "like a guy who makes his wife keep a scrapbook for him," Hamilton was not making fair use of the letter by changing the phrase to "the sort of fellow who makes his wife keep an album of his press cuttings." He was "tracking" Salinger's actual form of expression too closely, even where it included clichés. (Salinger used even the clichés, Judge Newman said, in his own unique, copyrighted way.)

Judge Newman also held that, to a certain extent, Hamilton's work might compete unfairly with any future commercial use Salinger wished to make of the letters, even though Hamilton's purpose was not to publish the letters themselves, but to provide the public (admittedly for a profit) with a scholarly work. "To deny the biographer like Hamilton the opportunity to copy the expressive content of unpublished letters is not," Judge Newman held, "to interfere in any significant way with the process of enhancing public knowledge of history or contemporary events. The facts may be reported." Hamilton's belief that the facts would sound "pedestrian" without their distinctive Salinger twist was, the judge added, of no legal moment.

It might be argued that, in his concern to protect Salinger, Judge Newman confounds copyright with privacy law. Judge Leval had found that "the wound [Salinger] has suffered is not from infringement of his copyright but from the publication of a biography that trespasses on his wish for privacy. The copyright law does not give him protection against that form of injury." (Nor, for that matter, would Hamilton's promises to the universities not to copy without permission.) For his part, Judge Leval might seem to entangle copyright law with his sympathy for the biographer's terrible dilemma: how, with any vibrancy, portray a literary man, a man distinctive for his literary style, without direct resort to the only available record of his life? How, in other words, could Hamilton follow the court's instructions and still honor his contract to provide "something new" — and monetarily profitable — about J.D. Salinger?

Judge Leval would have accorded greater First Amendment protection ("freedom of expression") to scholars and the reading public, where Judge Newman emphasizes individual legal right — leaving biographers and other scholars anxious that his strictures on the use of unpublished material will significantly cramp their style. Both arguments have a weighty attraction: serious readers and writers find themselves, in the words of Carol Rinzler, a lawyer who keeps a weather eye on copyright law for the publishing industry, "hard-pressed to decide which side they're on and equally hard-pressed not to sound silly while they make up their minds." On October 5, 1987, the United States Supreme Court denied Hamilton and Random House the right to appeal Judge Newman's decision. In 1988, Hamilton published his book, now called *In Search of J.D. Salinger* and more or less a recounting of his own struggles with the Salinger mythos, to mixed reviews.

In Canada, copyright law has protected an artist's reputation, if not his privacy, even where contracts were silent. *The Copyright Act* of 1921 in a sense extended contractual relations infinitely, when all commercial intercourse between the parties had long ceased. Under statute, it accorded a creator of a work something of the "moral" rights Salinger was seeking in his dispute with Ian Hamilton and Random House.

In 1982, for example, artist Michael Snow applied for an injunction under the *Copyright Act* to prevent the Eaton Centre mall from tampering with his "flight stop," one of the most pleasant works of public art in the city. Owned by Canada's largest department store chain, the Eaton Centre occupies an entire square block in Toronto's "Times Square" area — "the track" — on Yonge Street, and houses just about every style of shop and restaurant the city offers. "Flight stop," a mobile sculpture of sixty geese in various postures of aerobatics, is suspended from the translucent canopied ceiling in the mall "galleria," providing relief there to shoppers momentarily sighing skyward for surcease from high prices and materialism. When, in honor of the Christmas season in 1982, staff at the Centre decided to put the birds in the shopping spirit by tying ribbons around their necks, Snow sought his own relief in federal copyright law:

> *Section 12 (7):* Independently of the author's copyright, and even after the assignment, either wholly or partially, of the said copyright, the author has the right to claim authorship of the work, *as well as the right to restrain any distortion, mutilation or other modification of the work that would be prejudicial to his honour or reputation* [emphasis added].

The Eaton Centre, owners of the sculpture, resisted on constitutional grounds: it was arguable, for instance, that the federal copyright act could not grant civil rights — such as "honour and reputation" — "independently" of copyright, civil rights falling under the jurisdiction of the *provincial* governments. Alternatively, they suggested that insofar as section 12 (7) could be said to grant rights similar to those protected by libel law, Eaton's had not libeled Snow. The center's lawyer, William Miller, pointed out that Snow had sold the piece not to an art gallery, but to "what might be called a temple of Mammon"; Snow should not be surprised, in other words, that Centre management considered the sculpture part and parcel of the commercial environment. The ribbons were just a bit of fun, engaged in by those who *owned* the geese. It was not as if someone had visited the Louvre and "put a codpiece on the David."

But Justice Joseph O'Brien of the High Court of Ontario found that the *Copyright Act* granted rights beyond those protected by libel law, and that it was reasonable for Snow to feel himself prejudiced in the departments of honor and reputation. "The plaintiff," his lordship wrote, "is adamant in his belief that his naturalistic composition had been made to look ridiculous by the addition of ribbons and suggests it is not unlike dangling earrings from the Venus de Milo. While the matter is not undisputed, the plaintiff's opinion is shared by a number of other well-respected artists and people knowledgeable in his field." Justice O'Brien accepted this view of the *cognoscenti*, and ordered that Snow's geese be permitted to soar canopyward, unencumbered, more or less, by the material world.

Under copyright law, even sculptors such as Michael Snow can be "authors." Indeed, unless there exists some kind of agency or employment relationship, any creator of any work — a photographer, a painter, a composer — is, for legal purposes, the author of that work. Ownership of the copyright stops with the creator until she "assigns" it, or parts of it, under contract (by "licenses," just as a license to drive is an assignment of right to use public roads), to someone else. Where there is more than one author, copyright is shared among them.

There is no case on record of a Muse suing in copyright, inspiration being understood to *precede* legal authorship, as when we picture the Muse at a writer's ear. There are no legal consequences of inspiration until the author, himself, acts on it. Or at least that is usually the case, despite a 1927 anomaly where the supposed "author" proved even more inaccessible than J.D. Salinger, who will at least break his tombish silence to protect his privacy and reputation. In *Cummins v. Bond*, the "author" would not act at all, let alone sue on his own behalf. He had been dead for something like nineteen hundred years.

The most that could be said for his participation in the dispute at bar was that he seemed to be assigning his copyright either to one or both of the mortal litigants, or that he was entering an implied contract with them. His name, they claimed, was Cleophas, and he was a disciple of Jesus who, according to Luke, met the Christ on the Emmaus road.

Defendant Bond was an architect and ardent Christian spiritualist who swore that, as he was especially interested in archaeological work at the ancient abbey in Glastonbury, Cleophas had communicated with him through a medium. The medium was plaintiff Geraldine Cummins, who had introduced Bond to Cleophas in 1925 during séances in her London home. Fortunately, Cummins was skilled at automatic writing, for Cleophas conveyed his views on archaeology — and everything else — at the rate of more than thirteen hundred words an hour. He used many obscure and scholarly references unfamiliar to Cummins and spoke an indescribable language, which, for some reason, Cummins translated into a brand of English somewhere between Shakespearean and Miltonian — King James Bible, perhaps. After each séance, Bond would take the resulting manuscript home to punctuate it, put it into paragraphs and generally make it editorially presentable. He then published parts of the collected works, asserting at least a one-third share of ownership.

When Cummins objected, Bond baldly claimed joint authorship and, alternatively, that there could be no copyright in a work written in 1925 by someone who had died in perhaps AD 50. (He argued that since no man owned the work, Cummins had no legal right to stop him publishing the work in any way he wished, without her acquiescence.) With this last point, Chancery Justice Eve had some sympathy: "Recognizing as I do that I have no jurisdiction extending to the sphere in which [Cleophas] moves, I think I ought to confine myself . . . to individuals who were alive when the work first came into existence." He could not hold "that authorship and copyright rest with someone already domiciled on the other side of the inevitable river."

But his lordship did rule that Cummins was sole author. Despite evidence that Bond was seminal to the production of the document and felt himself to be a transformer of data between Cleophas and Geraldine Cummins (or a co-medium in the trinity-contract: for one thing, he, not Cummins, understood the terminology and history of the matters described), he was "labouring under a complete delusion in thinking that he in any way contributed" to the "automatic" writings. Bond seemed to have religious hallucinations, the judge said, and perhaps he was having legal ones as well. On her part, Geraldine Cummins was not Cleophas's "mere conduit pipe." (The more usual, and perhaps less Freudian, legal phrase is "mere amanuensis," a transcriber, such as one who takes notes of a lecture, the lecturer remaining the legal "author" of the words, though he *speaks* and it is the transcriber who *writes*.) Her contribution entailed considerable skill and imagination — extraordinary writing speed and "a peculiar ability to reproduce in archaic English matter communicated to her in some unknown tongue."

Of course, it could still be argued that there was some kind of contract between Cummins and Bond — perhaps that they would share the proceeds of the profits from what Cummins called "The Chronicles of Cleophas."

As was noted in Chapter Four, the common law seems to say that if a pseudonym is identified strongly with its user, it becomes that user's property. If a writer at the *Xanadu Post*, for instance, writes a column called "Holly's Household Hints," the paper cannot assign that name to another writer, or keep the original writer from using it, if it has become part of her "stock-in-trade."

This principle seems to have applied to "Joe Bob Briggs," the name under which John Bloom of the Dallas *Times Herald* became a foul-mouthed, red-neck drive-in-movie reviewer. When controversy erupted and the column was canceled, the newspaper tried to stop Bloom from publishing a collection of the columns as his own property, but then capitulated. Insofar as Joe Bob and Bloom were one and the same, the stock-in-trade principle says that Bloom's rights to his nom de plume would not cease with the termination of his employment contract.

During his more than three years at the newspaper, Joe Bob — John Bloom in a persona that his colleagues wouldn't have associated with him in a million years — tenaciously proved himself "an equal opportunity offender." In an age self-conscious with "feminism," he insisted on calling women bimbos, even those who wrote him fan letters. And he was extravagantly more impressed by their "garbonzas" than their brains. He denigrated homosexuals and, in a column he called "We Are the Weird," a column which very nearly ended his career, he did call some black people "stupid Negroes."

His editors should not have allowed it: whatever Bloom's intent, the words had too much potential to hurt and anger. But as he pointed out in a column comparing Joe Bob's demise at the *Herald* to the deaths of John Kennedy and Abe Lincoln ("Lincoln and Kennedy were both assassinated on a Friday. Joe Bob was assassinated on a Tuesday. Makes you think"), in that same piece Joe Bob had said "stupid white people" twice. And from one perspective, the point of his deliberate outrages was criticism not of movies but of white, good-ol'-boy bigotry.

An aloof, intelligent son of Southern Baptist schoolteachers ("fellow

Babtists," as Joe Bob would call them), Bloom proved himself a strong starter when the *Times Herald* hired him away from a country-club magazine in 1981. He was first assigned "fluff-and-filler" features, but soon took on more serious investigative reporting, including — as Calvin Trillin pointed out in a *New Yorker* Joe Bob story in 1986 — essays on the Ku Klux Klan and on the plight of local Mexican-Americans.

Bloom moved briefly to the *Texas Monthly*, then returned to the *Times Herald* as its movie reviewer. Shortly thereafter, a features editor asked him to write something on the popularity of drive-in movie theaters in Dallas, the hook being that in many other centers in the U.S., the drive-in was on the skids. That was how Joe Bob Briggs was born.

In an introductory column, Bloom claimed to have met him in the popcorn line at an all-night Bela Lugosi marathon. He traded Joe Bob an unbuttered popcorn for a buttered Tub o' Corn, Joe Bob fuming that the Tub would get grease on the upholstery of his '68 baby-blue Dodge Dart, "which actually he didn't buy until '76." Joe Bob was so grateful, he condescended to sit with Bloom in the lawn-chair section of the drive-in. (Later, Briggs would write a "Guide to Impeccable Drive-In Etiquette" which, along with a warning not to order Mexican food at a drive-in, advised that the aficionado should never bring lawn chairs. "The worst you can do is take up space somebody could've used to park in.") There, Joe Bob told Bloom "all the scenes of *Zombies on Broadway* before they happened," and explained that, although he was only nineteen (an assertion Bloom doubted) and had been married three times, he had already watched 6,800 drive-in movies.

Bloom told Calvin Trillin something more revealing. He had been kicking the Joe Bob idea around with his editor for some time, asking him "what would happen if a movie critic loved *I Spit on Your Grave* and hated *Dumbo*" — had "started looking at Charles Bronson as an *auteur?*"

Joe Bob's *schtick*, a description he would never use, is the sort of commentary you'd expect to hear trailing along a string of beer-and-taco belches. His professional credo contains statements such as "I only approve of gratuitous nudity when it's necessary to the story. *Or* when it's a real boring movie and you need some nekkid women to liven things up." His first review was of *The Grim Reaper*. In it he mildly approved of the plot "about a guy who will use a meat cleaver when he has to, but usually he just uses his mouth," but he didn't even approach what was to become the quintessential Joe Bob review.

The quintessential Joe Bob review almost always includes autobiographical details only tangentially related to the movie under consideration, details mostly about Joe Bob's tumultous relationships with women who have the intelligence of a "box of rocks." And the quintessential Joe Bob always ends with a summary, giving a tally of everything from naked female breasts on display (alive, maimed and dead), to car chases to kung-fu fights and other violence (for example, "one bimbo neck impaled on wire"), corpses, rolling heads and "beasts." As well, Joe Bob characteristically includes useful facetiae such as (in a review of *High Test Girls*), "No plot to get in the way. Excellent dubbed moaning. . . Three stars. Joe Bob says check it out."

Several Dallas feminists counted themselves among the millions of fans who picked Joe Bob up in syndication — success unanticipated by his now very nervous editors, who had groggily allowed him into the *Times Herald* via a largely unread Friday supplement. According to Trillin, these feminists thought Joe Bob really had "served to demonstrate just how ludicrous Texas he-men were."

But one of them, Charlotte Taft, president of the local NOW chapter and director of a Dallas abortion clinic, finally did take umbrage, at Joe Bob's glorification of the schlock-gore *Pieces*. Joe Bob had encapsulated it as "All on-camera chain-saw deaths are absolutely necessary to the plot. Heads roll twice. Arms roll. Legs roll. . . . Nine living breasts, two dead breasts. . . . Splatter City. Four stars."

Taft organized a postcard protest campaign, which Joe Bob baptized "Attack of the Mushmouth French-Fry Heads." He pointed out that he had enormous respect for women, "especially when they have garbonzas the size of Cleveland," and that he was violently opposed to the use against women of chain saws, power drills, tire tools, rubber hoses, brass knuckles, "bob wire," hypodermics, embalming needles and poleaxes "unless it is *necessary* to the plot."

He also took the opportunity to reply to one of Taft's allies, a columnist at the *Times Herald*'s much more conventional rival, the *Morning*

News. The columnist had compared Joe Bob to Mother Teresa, and it was no contest until Joe Bob mounted an extended personal assault ("Joe Bob Attacked by Communist Friend of Mother Teresa") on the columnist's appearance ("his eyes look exactly like the guy in *I Drink Your Blood*"). Joe Bob ended his reply by challenging Charlotte Taft to a nude mud-wrestling match.

Perceiving that she was only playing into Joe Bob's hands (this was the man, after all, who declared a movie a success if it was "Better Than *E. T.* in the Garbonza Department"), Taft withdrew from the battlefield. But she later told Trillin that, considering how hard times were for abortion clinics, especially on the financial front, "sometimes she thinks she might have been too quick in rejecting Joe Bob's mud-wrestling match."

Others were more persistent. Before his sudden demise, Joe Bob had also worked as a sports reporter for the *Times Herald*, a job the editors seemed to hope would channel Bloom's wicked talent into safer areas. But by Christmastime, 1985 and the "We Are the World" phenomenon — the charity movement in aid of starving Africans, inspired by music and a video recorded by rock stars — it became apparent, to the *Times Herald* editors, at least, that Joe Bob was their resident Frankenstein.

Around that time, Joe Bob reported "Joe Bob, Drive-In Artists Join Forces for Minorities with 'We Are the Weird,'" asserting forthrightly that he wasn't getting "a penny out of this except 35 percent raked off the top." The great philanthropist Leatherface had been on hand, as had mass murderer Jason from the *Hallowe'en* movies, the Swamp Thing, Pia Zadora and Charles Bronson, all arm in arm ("except for The Mutant, who don't have no arms"), swaying and "singin' their little hearts out." You could say the song itself was an attack on human inhumanity, or inequitable distribution of wealth — or you could say it was an attack on self-inflated rock stars, albeit an attack with a very blunt instrument:

There comes a time
When we need a piece of meat
When the world
Must scrape together some grub

There are Negroes dying
And it's time to make em eat
They don't really need no Nutra-Sweet.

We are the weird,
We are the starvin,
We are the scum of the filthy earth,
So let's start scarfin.
There's a goat-head bakin
We're calling it their food,
If the Meskins can eat it,
They can eat it too.

Bloom's editors, like many readers, would later claim that they had become so inured to Joe Bob's outrageousness that no alarm bells went off, even when he said that "We Are the Weird" had been recorded to benefit minority groups in Africa and the United Negro College Fund at home, "cause I think we should be sending as many Negroes to college as we can, specially the stupid Negroes." When several hundred people marched on the offices of the *Times Herald*, and the paper's black employees complained of group defamation, editor Will Jarrett killed the Joe Bob movie column on the spur of the moment. The next day, he ran a front-page apology.

Bloom, who was out of town giving a speech, flat resigned from the *Times Herald*, furious at Jarrett's precipitous back-pedal. He plainly felt that free expression was a condition of his contract of employment. And of course when Bloom collected the Joe Bob columns in a book, the *Times Herald* could not say with a straight face that the Joe Bob name had great commercial value for them which Bloom was co-opting. It was true that Bloom had invented the character while under contract to the *Times Herald*, but how could the paper's publishers claim Joe Bob as valuable property — a trademark on loan to Bloom as long as he worked for the *Times Herald* — while holding their noses and putting a gun to his head?

At this writing, Joe Bob is still in syndication, but his audience has shrunk dramatically. Bloom also tours him as a one-man show.

In some instances where a contract is breached, a plaintiff will seek to have it "specifically enforced" instead of requesting money damages. If, in other words, Shylock loans Antonio money and accepts a pound of Antonio's flesh as collateral, a court order of "specific performance" on the contract would mean that Antonio must suffer himself to be mutilated (assuming he doesn't pay the debt in time and ignoring the fact that it is illegal as "against public policy" to contract to harm someone); he couldn't just pay the value of that flesh. If Antonio fails to repay the loan, he must give *specifically* what he promised he would give.

At common law, however, a court will not award specific performance for a *personal service contract* unless the defendant has promised *not* to do something. The courts prefer to give money damages rather than force people, in the manner of legalized slavery, to do things against their will. In a famous case, Warner Brothers once sued Bette Davis for walking out of her contract with them in the United Kingdom to take movie roles in the United States. While the Court of King's Bench would not enforce a clause in the contract that obliged Davis "to perform solely and exclusively" for Warner Brothers, it did hold her to a promise *not* to "render any services for or in any phonographic, stage or motion picture production or productions or business . . . or engage in any other occupation without the written consent of the producer." The court reasoned that enforcing the contract's "negative provisions" was not the same as forcing Davis to perform her contract. She would "be able to employ herself both usefully and remuneratively in other spheres of activity, though not as remuneratively as in her special line. She will not be driven, although she may be tempted, to perform the contract."

In an 1833 precedent, however, when a New York theater had contracted with an Italian *primo basso* "to sing, gesticulate, and recite . . . in all operas, serious, semi-serious and comic, farces, oratorios, concerts, cantatas and benefits," and appear at all rehearsals as required, the New York Court of Chancery had used quasi-criminal law remedies to enforce the more commonplace dictum that the show must go on. When the theater manager learned that the singer was planning to leave for Havana, he had the singer thrown in debtor's prison under a writ of *ne exeat* — an order to the sheriff requiring him to jail a person until that person puts up bail to secure a promise not to leave the jurisdiction of the court. The chancellor of the court admitted that no court official "possesses that exquisite sensibility in the auricular nerve which is necessary to understand, and to enjoy with a proper zest, the peculiar beauties of the Italian opera." Nor could a judicial officer assure *specific* performance in light of the "effect coercion might produce upon the defendant's singing, especially in livelier airs," and in light of the fact that "the fear of imprisonment would unquestionably deepen his seriousness in the graver parts of the drama." He ordered the release of the prisoner ("his songs will be neither comic, or even semi-serious, while he remains confined in that dismal cage"), but, remarking that "a bird that can sing and will not sing must be made to sing," added that he would reconsider remedies if the man insisted on breaching his contract.

If there is law here, it is not good law. To get around the fact that, while releasing the prisoner, the chancellor baldly misstates the rule on personal service contracts ("I suppose it must be conceded that the complainant is entitled to specific performance"), the American contract authority Corbin gives the judgment a paradoxical and undeservedly liberal reading. Corbin finds that the chancellor's labored attempts to show how the court could not *assure* specific performance (because the court was not expert on opera, and because coercion and threats would make it impossible for the singer to perform in his accustomed manner) somehow release the singer from performing as he'd agreed. The fact is, the singer's predicament is an even more extreme instance of Hobson's choice than Bette Davis's case. Bette Davis at least wins the choice to stand on her principles, however materially pinching she might find the consequences.

What, again, if the tables were turned? What if a singer felt perfectly happy with his contract but the theater burned down before he could honor it? That issue came up inferentially 30 years later when the Surrey Gardens and Music Hall was destroyed by fire before impresarios Taylor and Lewis could use it under contract. The team had planned a real extravaganza, "a series of four grand concerts and day and night fetes," featuring military bands, al fresco entertainments of various descriptions; coloured minstrels; fireworks and full illuminations; a ballet or divertissement, if permitted; a wizard and Grecian statues; tight rope performances; rifle galleries; air gun shooting; Chinese and Parisian games; boats on the lake,

as well as any other activities Taylor would dream up. The star turn of the concerts was to be, as the conclusion of the contract itself put it, "Mr. Sims Reeves, God's will permitting."

When the theater was reduced to skeleton and ash and the impresarios added insult to injury by suing its owners for loss of profits, the owners relied heavily on this last clause. The fire had been an act of God. There was no breach of contract, because "God's will" had not permitted its discharge.

The great legal scholar Sir Frederick Pollock has suggested that the clause was in the way of a joke, or sardonicism, and could not have been meant as a true condition; tenor John Sims Reeves, it seems, sang only when the mood took him, balking if he thought performance would compromise the long-term quality of his "instrument." Pollock declares himself on Reeves's side; by saving his voice and disappointing the occasional few, Reeves assured that a whole "younger generation" was able to hear him later in his life.

If the court itself cared about the meaning of the "God's will permitting" clause, it didn't say so. The judge, Sir Colin Blackburn, kept his eye firmly on the material world, holding that at the time of making the contract, the parties must have assumed the concert hall would continue to exist through the period agreed upon: existence of the hall was an *implied condition* of their bargain. It was the same case as when you agree to sell a horse or a slave but then the horse or slave sickens and dies. Unless you were somehow responsible for the death, you could not be held accountable for it. (History does not record whether Sims Reeves approved of the comparison.) The contract to rent the hall was frustrated, and both parties were left as they had been before it was made.

In a sense, Geraldine Cummins, the medium and stenographer in the "Chronicles of Cleophas" case, might be said to have been the *agent* of the disembodied Cleophas, his lieutenant in literary matters. Paradoxically, among the strictly mortal, the agency relationship can seem even more metaphysical.

In 1987, for example, Gio Hernandez would not necessarily have described himself as an agent, professionally, or at least specifically; but on the other hand, he probably would not have ruled the characterization completely out. As a "hair-stylist" at the fashionable Bergdorf-Goodman department store in New York, and later in a shop of his own, Hernandez saw himself as a Figaro sort of barber, friend and matchmaker to the rich and powerful. Many fellow New Yorkers shared this view, although some of them eventually concluded that Gio was a Figaro sort of barber in the sense that he wanted to bleed you. But the dispute between Gio and these disgruntleds had nothing to do with tonsorial history — which says that the barber's pole is a relic of the day he gave his clients a staff to clutch while he *surgically* bled them, the stripes representing the gory dressings and the knob at the top representing the basin which caught the gore. Rather, at stake was whether Gio had in fact acted as Lee Iacocca's literary agent.

There was no express agreement to that effect — no "Gio is to act as Lee's literary agent" typed out in triplicate. Everybody admitted that Gio had cut the Chrysler chairman's hair, and that he had performed similar services for the vice-president of marketing at Bantam Books, Stuart Applebaum. They also admitted that he was the Figaro sort of barber he held himself out to be, at least insofar as he was the *factotum della citta*, factotum, commiserator, confidant, adviser and facilitator for just about everyone who was anyone in New York. Which was to say that you were nobody unless Gio Hernandez cut your hair — and, incidentally, did you favors.

All parties agreed that Gio acted as a go-between to help get Lee interested in doing a book for Stuart — a biography that eventually grossed a record-breaking dozen or so million dollars, at last public accounting. Everyone agreed, as well, that though Bantam sent its biggest guns after Lee, for many months he held fast against going literary. Gio Hernandez would later say that Stuart Applebaum promised him a commission from the start, if, with Lee captive to Gio's clippers and razor, he could bend Lee's ear in Bantam's direction.

Gio did just that, although Bantam has since suggested that Gio wanted a commission only *after Iacocca* proved to be a blockbuster. Still, to promote the book, Bantam eagerly used the story about Gio as Figaroid go-between, invited Gio to the launch party and eventually offered him a $5,000 "finder's fee."

Gio told another customer about the finder's fee. That customer was fractious lawyer Roy Cohn, himself often at trouble's ear (Cohn was counsel to Senator Joseph McCarthy's anti-Communism hearings in the 1950s, and during his controversial career was acquitted of bribery, conspiracy, extortion, blackmail and other charges), Cohn told Gio $5,000 "was no better than a tip for a haircut," and Gio seems to have been inclined to agree. Stuart Applebaum had promised him "a lot of money," he said. Before Cohn died in 1986, he filed an action against Bantam on Gio's behalf, alleging fraud and breach of contract and claiming for Gio the agent's conventional ten percent — something on the order of $1.2 million.

When the case reaches trial, Gio's new lawyer might like to quote that other barber case, *Vann v. Ionta* (Chapter Four), which assessed whether another New York hairstylist showed "reckless" propensities — whether he rendered his customers so giddy with laughter that they mindlessly grabbed at his razor. Jimmie the barber was held blameless there because, from Roman times, barbers have always been, if not song-and-dance men, at least more than just hairstylists:

> That Figaro acquits himself nobly in all his missions [as matchmaker, surgeon, adviser, agent, druggist, wig-maker, barber . . .] demonstrates that the present barber's predecessor was a genial and astute fellow with courageous directness . . . He is a high-class salesman.

A barber can be a Fortune 500 guy's best friend. Whether he is his agent, time will tell.

At bottom, of course, the "Jimmie-the-Joking-Barber" case was a different sort of agency problem, the question there being twofold: had Jimmie been negligent in "fooling around with the customers"; and, was his boss, Rose Ionta, responsible for that negligence by the doctrine that a master is responsible for the foreseeable misbehavior of the servant? The court read into the contract between barber and customer an implied term: with his shave and haircut, the customer was apt to get a little song-and-dance thrown into the bargain. Jimmie's exuberance was customary in his profession, not negligent or reckless.

It would seem to follow then, that if you go to a strip joint and fall while ogling an act, you have no remedy in tort or contract: no doubt about it, with your "cover charge" and refreshment payments, you bargain for food, drink and the opportunity to see naked women "shake that thing." If you watch them instead of your step, that's your problem.

But that wasn't how the Alberta Court of Queen's Bench saw it in 1983 when a Mr. Edwards tripped over the steps at Tracy Starr's restaurant in Edmonton and ended up crippled for the rest of his life. Again, and as often happens, the law of contract and the law of tort were mixed and mingled — and blended, it seems, with emotional matters external to the law proper. At least in reading *Edwards v. Tracy Starr's*, you have to wonder if the court was swayed less by its feeling for the law than the picture of an unusually sympathetic plaintiff taking on a defendant some may have viewed as immoral.

Edwards had held security guard and administrative jobs in Prince Albert, Saskatchewan, having been rendered unfit for other sorts of work after an army accident in 1954, when premature detonation of an explosive tore away his left hand and the use of his left eye. He had recently retired, and was visiting his daughter and son-in-law in Edmonton at the time of his fall. By the end of the evening at Tracy Starr's with his son-in-law (the wives were at bingo), he had ruptured the quadriceps muscles in both his legs and would require braces and canes to walk. In many ways, he was rendered helpless.

It was true that both he and his son-in-law had used the aisle where he would fall, and that the entertainers, waitresses and other patrons navigated it night after night. Edwards had consumed two, maybe three drinks, but also dinner: the court accepted his testimony that he was not "impaired." The bill had been paid. Edwards and his son-in-law had returned from the men's room and were about to leave when he tripped over a step obtruding into the aisle. The step led up to the stage, where the naked woman was honoring her contract of employment and Edwards was directing his attention.

The way the court saw it, "there was an unfortunate combination of an existing obstacle or hazard and a distraction at the crucial time. Both were provided by the proprietor." In other words, it was Tracy Starr's fault that Edwards was not looking where he was going! "He was not doing so because he was distracted by the nude female on stage. The occupier [Starr's] put her there to be looked at and, in my view, cannot say the visitor should not have allowed himself to be distracted." Distraction was on offer as part of the contract. The court awarded Edwards something around $195,000, including $15,000 in trust for his wife in return for the care she had provided Edwards during the four years between the accident and the trial.

As in *Donoghue v. Stevenson*, tort was used here to limit the scope of freedom of contract, or at least the range of situations it will cover. Again, it seems that courts will meld tort and contract — attach a finding of negligence to what, legally, is otherwise a contract dispute — where a strictly commercial remedy, in breach of contract, is not conventionally available. The same forces operate in the other landlord-user litigation discussed in Chapter Five — the *Rush* rotten privy case, the "falling armchair" case, the "locked loo" case, and so on. (As in those instances, the question in *Edwards* amounts to "Who was the proximate cause of the plaintiff's injury — the plaintiff, the landlord or someone else?") Instead of bluntly finding that Edwards should have watched his step or that his contract with Starr's did not include risk of physical harm, the law plays the political game of commercial conservatism, protecting the sanctity of contract while expressing establishment disdain for a certain kind of business. The disdain is behind-the-hand, of course, euphemized: it is conventionally acceptable for a cola company to "diversify" into bomb making, for restaurant chains and publishing companies to destroy rain forests, even for nearly naked women to appear in commercials selling beer, as long as these enterprises are run quietly, under the companies' traditional "public relations" veneer. Businessmen may visit strip bars at lunch, but by and large they do not recognize the landlord as a professional peer.

CHAPTER EIGHT

Patients and Doctors,
Morons and Bankers,
Students and Teachers

"Medical malpractice" usually connotes tort harm — negligence, or, less often, battery (the doctor "touches" you without your informed consent, "touching" being understood in a broad sense and including surgery or any other treatment). Although the physician-patient relationship is largely a commercial one, nobody uses "malpractice" to mean "contract damages." The reasons are psychological and cultural: although we pay for medical care, our doctors are our most powerful intimates — not friends and benefactors, nor even co-conspirators against decay and death, but our saviors. In these materialistic times, physicians themselves struggle with the paradox: are they businesspeople or shamans?

More pragmatically, the law prefers tort over contract remedies in physician-patient relationships because, to paraphrase a leading U.S. case on the subject, doctors cannot *make promises* about treatment with any great certainty. There are too many vagaries, too many unknowns about an individual patient's susceptibilities or idiosyncracies. Juries and judges should not be asked to believe, this line of argument goes, that a reasonable doctor would promise complete success. Whatever their pretensions to omnipotence, doctors are not gods.

(There remains the fact, as well, that the judiciary is even more reluctant to interfere in professional bargains, which are technically complicated and are made by members of the judges' own social class, than they are to interfere in purely commercial ones. As is evident in *Edwards v. Tracy Starr's*, physical injury relating to a business practice is normally categorized as a tort or quasi-tort problem instead of as a contract matter.)

Still, in that very case, for three "nose jobs" that went wrong on one unfortunate woman, the court found the doctor in breach of contract — with special mention that the patient was in show business, and that the doctor *promised* to give her a certain type of nose. According to the opinion, the nose he eventually did give her had a dent in it, a bulbous front and an asymmetrical tip. The patient was awarded damages for what she spent on the treatment, and also for the "worsening of her condition" and for any physical and mental suffering that went beyond what she would have endured had the operations been successful.

This case follows the reasoning on both the contract and damages issues in a famous older suit, the so-called "hairy hand case," heard by the New Hampshire Supreme Court in 1929. *Hawkins v. McGee*, collected in virtually every contract law casebook and featured in the popular novel and movie *The Paper Chase*, is a case about a skin graft performed on the palm of the hand of a young man who, nine years before, had been burned by an electric wire. According to the young man, George Hawkins, and his father, Dr. Edward McGee had promised to remove a mass of scar tissue that had accumulated on the palm and, by skin-grafts, to give Hawkins a hand that was as good as new. The doctor implored the Hawkinses for some time to try a graft, as he wanted to gain experience with the treatment himself. When the Hawkinses at last agreed, McGee removed the scar tissue, then stitched young George Hawkins's hand to his chest, forcing him to walk bent over for three or four weeks. Once the hand was separated from the thorax and the bandages removed, the now-pinched skin on Hawkins's chest (a patch of it having been cut out for the hand) made it difficult for Hawkins to stand straight, and the hand had a new sort of mass in it. Some sources say the mass resembled a hair transplant. During direct examination by his lawyer in court, Hawkins testified that "if I was introduced to somebody I had never known before, and go to shake hands with him, and especially a woman, they want to know what is in my hand. . . . It is embarrassing. The fellows have a good time making jokes about it."

According to the Hawkinses, in talking them into the operation, McGee had said, "I will guarantee to make the hand a hundred per-cent perfect hand or a hundred percent good hand." But McGee suggested to the jury that "even if these words were uttered by him, no reasonable man would understand that they were used with the intention of entering 'into any contractual relation whatever.'" He had merely been giving a professional *opinion*, not a promise or warranty. It was essentially the same defense that would find judicial approval, at least in principle, as late as 1973 in the nose-job case. For that matter, at the time it already carried the impressive weight of more than 300 years of common law authority, from the day in 1602 that a man named Lopus sued a goldsmith for selling him "bad drugs."

Lopus thought he was buying a "bezoar stone," a concretion that was thought to have medicinal qualities, despite the fact that it was fished from the guts of dead animals, where it was formed of "layers of animal matter deposited around some foreign substance" the animal had ingested. Lopus's stone did not meet this definition, and he sued. This was long before the days of Mrs. Wallis and her nice crabs for tea, of course, and the courts held that the stone carried no *implied* warranty (or guarantee) that it would be fit for Lopus's purpose: caveat emptor, more or less. Lopus could get his money back only if the goldsmith, Chandelor, had been deliberately lying when he told Lopus the stone was a bezoar. Otherwise, his only remedy was to start a rock collection.

On such reasoning, the law today would oblige a bridegroom to keep a piece of glass that a jeweller inadvertently sold him as the Hope diamond. Yet, according to the nose-job case, in certain instances the *Chandelor* rule of caveat emptor can apply to *physician-patient transactions*. (It didn't in the nose-job case because of the doctor's express promise to a special patient, an actress.) Absent fraud, goldsmith Chandelor was giving only his opinion, not a guarantee that the stone would be a bezoar. Similarly, in giving an optimistic prognosis, a physician does not automatically guarantee one-hundred-percent success for his treatments.

Nonetheless, the jury in *Hawkins v. McGee* found for young George

Hawkins: they held the doctor to what they decided was an express guarantee to give George a perfectly smooth (hairless) palm. Such is the beauty of the lay jury: they did not know, or care, about the 300 years of common law founded on *Chandelor v. Lopus*. If for three centuries the law had been nervous about moving away from caveat emptor, shifting some moral burden onto the "seller" (here, the provider of medical services), they felt no such reluctance.

When McGee appealed, the Supreme Court held that the jury was entitled to find as it did, but that the trial court had instructed them incorrectly on the matter of damages. The trial judge was wrong, the Supreme Court said, to tell the jury that it could give damages for pain and suffering *per se*:

> The pain necessarily incident to a serious surgical operation was a part of the contribution which the plaintiff was willing to make to his joint undertaking with the defendant to produce a good hand. It was a legal detriment suffered by him which constituted a part of the consideration given by him for the contract. It represented a part of the price which he was willing to pay for a good hand.

Unavoidable pain and suffering were, in effect, part of the medical bill. As the Hawkinses refused to accept this view and insisted on full damages for George's suffering, the case was sent back to superior court for a new trial. But before it was heard, the parties settled for $1,400. When Dr. McGee attempted to claim that amount from his insurers, they refused to pay out, on the ground (ironically) that he was not insured for such "special contracts." This may have been an instance of at least poetic justice: on appeal, the doctor had attacked Hawkins's original victory by saying that the jury had wrongfully discussed the likelihood that McGee was covered by malpractice insurance. (Conventional legal wisdom says that if jury-members believe a defendant has insurance, they will inflate the damages they award the plaintiff. For this reason, the law of evidence often forbids juries to consider insurance coverage.) He implied, in other words, that the jury found as it did for Hawkins not for legal reasons but because it had decided that McGee's insurance company, instead of McGee personally, would have to pay any damages.

Hawkins is a useful law-school primer on contract basics,

demonstrating how the nature of a binding promise, and the extent to which the promise is enforceable, have remained legally contentious throughout history. Perhaps even more suggestively, it shows that consideration, as a modern refinement in contract law, has become an especially abstruse ground of contention, spawning last-resort arguments when all others fail. (In *Hawkins*, the primary argument is about what the doctor *promised*; the *pain-and-suffering* consideration issue relates to George Hawkins's *damages*, cropping up only after the court has defined the promise.) Where in 1929 it seemed abstract to consider pain part of the consideration for the contract, part of the "cost" of an operation, today we accept that suffering is "merchantable," or at least occasionally compensable even in contract damages, and instead we haggle over what kinds of suffering count, and to what extent. While, according to the *Ruffolo* suit against Prime Minister Mulroney and the Canadian Progressive Conservatives, voter disillusionment is not a "compensable head of damages," refraining from swearing and smoking can count, as can breathing the effusions of a smoke ball. "Consideration" has become so broad a category that some scholars argue its expansion has helped destroy the classical idea of contract.

During the eighteenth century, the influential English judge and law reformer, Lord Mansfield, made a heroic attempt to simplify contract law by declaring consideration to be peripheral: consideration, his lordship suggested, need not have passed to make deals binding; it merely served as evidence of the serious intent of the bargaining parties. But as life in general has become more complicated, "consideration" has become a grab-bag of judicial responses — here an excuse, there a hedge, elsewhere the only choice. A case as recent as two years ago demonstrates, on both its law and facts, how decisively Lord Mansfield's suggestion has been snubbed — how, in fact, it was doomed by the immense social and commercial pressures of the expanding industrial economy. At the same time, it challenges the notion of a "classical contract" form, shifting the very mundane practice of barter firmly into metaphysics.

Whether this was the original intention of J.S.G. Boggs, a thirty-two-year-old American artist living in London, remains ambiguous. For several years, Boggs had made his living as a "numeric artist," as he described himself, an enterprise that began with paintings "playing with numbers" and eventually led Boggs to buy goods and services with his meticulously rendered drawings of paper money.

In exchange for a seventy-five-cent cup of coffee, for example, Boggs might offer a drawing of a dollar bill. In Switzerland, he managed to pay for his room at the five-star Hotel Euler and to buy four shirts in this way. When cab drivers discovered his money drawings could fetch as much as ten times their face value, they raced through the streets of Basel trying to score him as their next fare.

In the fall of 1986, at a Blackfriars gallery called The Young Unknowns, Boggs mounted a show of the fruits of these labors, each work comprising three parts: first, the drawing of the paper currency Boggs used in a transaction, perfectly imitated with only small details changed (Boggs having substituted his signature for a treasury official's, or a self-portrait for that of a sovereign; Boggs playing with an official slogan: "This note is legal tender for artists"); second, the change he demanded as if he were making the purchase with "real" money (the currency signed by Boggs and the coins etched with his initials); and third, the receipt. In one older work, he included, as well, the four Swiss shirts. His usual practice was to say nothing about the transaction for twenty-four hours, to give the other party time to think about it. Then, if collectors wanted to track the drawing down, Boggs sold them the receipt and change, building one transaction atop the other. He charged extra for the name of the person who made the original deal with him. The drawing was then usually framed with the receipt and signed change.

In a piece about Boggs and his 1986 show, the legal correspondent for the *Daily Telegraph* drew all of Britain's attention to Section 18 of the 1981 *Forgery and Counterfeiting Act*, which makes it an offense "to reproduce," without the permission of the Bank of England, "on any substance whatsoever, and whether or not to correct scale, any British currency note." Reading this, Boggs decided he should write to the Bank of England for permission to continue drawing and exhibiting his versions of pound notes, but the Bank refused to look at his work, or even to talk to his lawyer.

Boggs wrote again, and again the bank rebuffed him. But he remained undeterred, even after Scotland Yard raided the Young Unknowns gallery, arrested him and confiscated all his work displayed there. The Yard held him for five and a half hours, during which he gave investigating detectives several Socratic lessons on art versus copying. (When, for example, a policeman asked Boggs if he had drawn or painted the seized works, he replied by asking if a dreamer is responsible for the creation of his own dreams.) In the end, the police declined to press charges.

But the imperious Bank of England was not so accommodating. On January 5, 1987, the bank instituted a private prosecution against Boggs in Horseferry Magistrates' Court. Three weeks later he elected trial by jury, and on April 8 he was committed for trial at the Old Bailey.

Although Boggs never represents his freehand money drawings to be anything other than his own artwork, they are so astonishingly detailed and precise that they have commanded increasingly high prices. Of course, his arrest and prosecution gave an enormous boost to his marketability. And his ascending worth on the artistic stock exchange, itself part of the phenomenon he toys with by the nature of his "numeric" art, produced the added wrinkle that other artists began forging his work and signature. In November 1987, the *Times* reported that a "Boggs" five-pound note had recently been offered for sale while the "real thing" sat in his lawyer's safe, having been paid by Boggs in lieu of legal fees. By then, Boggs had decided that his art included not only the drawing, and not even the drawing and the barter he made with it, but everything stimulated by, that transaction.

Throughout his legal troubles Boggs insisted that what he was doing was not reproduction (especially as that term is understood by artists) but art. When the Bank of England decided to press for a fine instead of a prison sentence, Boggs remarked with some calm that he would probably end up in prison anyway. He would insist on paying the fine in drawings, he said, and would then probably be committed for contempt. "I am trying to preserve the freedom of artistic expression," he declared, "and I would rather go to prison than compromise what I believe in."

This was not mere bravado, for the case against him looked daunting. His lead barrister, civil rights dynamo Geoffrey Robertson, did not expect to win until an appeal all the way to the European Commission on Human Rights. Boggs's trial at the Old Bailey on four days in November 1987, during which a tipstaff ordered him to stop "reproducing" the coat of arms over the Bench, seemed to prove these expectations. Defender Robertson took the position of the Court of Chancery in *Morning Star Co-Operative Soc. v. Express Newspapers* that "only a moron in a hurry" would mistake Boggs's drawings for genuine currency of the realm. (In *Morning Star*, the court had ruled that only a moron in a hurry would confuse a racy "titty tabloid" called the *Daily Star* with the broadsheet-style tract newspaper — formerly *The Daily Worker* — published by the Communist plaintiffs.)

This apparently led to some remarkable advocacy, including examination of witnesses by the prosecution as to how much confusion would be in the air if a moron in a hurry viewed Boggs's drawings *in a dimly-lit room*. The bank's witnesses proved unflappable, and the judge, Sir David McNeill, summed up firmly against Boggs. It was no defense that the drawings "may be worth more than the originals," his lordship said. Reproduction was reproduction as every thinking adult understood it.

The jury was out for no more than fifteen minutes, and reported that only a moron in a black mood would convict J.S.G. Boggs of contravening the *Forgery and Counterfeiting Act*. Or, anyway, as twelve of his peers, they unanimously found him not guilty. Outside the Old Bailey, a triumphant Boggs displayed a new drawing he had worked at after the tipstaff scolded him for sketching the courtroom — a rendition of a fifty-pound note.

Is it fair, or artistic, or ethical, to say that your art contains everything it simulates? Isn't art supposed to be deliberately selective instead of random and transactional? Isn't it antithetical to the idea of "art" that the environment controls the artist instead of vice versa? Isn't there a difference between artistic originality and shocking people with, and out of, the ordinary? Is the collector of Boggs's art, in other words, getting value for money — consideration for consideration!? However we might feel about the legitimacy of such "transactional art," Boggs does make us step back from the everyday barter — *two removes* back when we shift from the original transaction to the transactions made by collectors on the hunt for Boggs's drawings: puzzles within puzzles — and focus on the many intangibles and leaps of faith in our money economy, not to mention in the feverish art market. He makes us see the relativity of "consideration": anything is "valuable consideration" if a sufficient number of people think it is. Sometimes, that sufficient number is one, the person accepting one sort of peppercorn — or "pined newt," as the title of one of Boggs's pound-note works has it — over another. Some people will pay tens of thousands of dollars for paintings by chimpanzees. Manhattan Island, some say, once changed ownership for a handful of beads and trinkets. Money itself is only paper, after all, and who is to say that promissory notes, stocks, bonds, mortgages — or refraining from smoking and swearing, or expecting fresh nutcakes for tea — aren't even more artificial than Boggs's highly skilled trompe-l'oeil?

The Bank of England v. Boggs perhaps proves the irreducible subjectivity of the everyday bargain: if two people agree that a piece of paper is valuable consideration, it is their perfect right to barter with it — a view that would have found favor at the dawn of our civilization twenty-five hundred years ago, with the Greek philosopher Protagoras, himself the proponent of a contract problem that awaits a satisfying solution. As *Boggs* stands as a summing-up at the end of this history of promises, Protagoras and his problem tie the beginning of that history to its end.

An Athenian jurist of wealth and standing, Protagoras boasted several firsts, including first sophist in the original sense of "professional teacher," and first person to have his books burned: in 415 BC he was expelled from Athens as an agnostic. He believed only in what he could discover with his senses. Thus, his motto, "Man is the measure of all things," is generally taken to mean that human experience is subjective or relative (whether one or the other is another matter of inkpot hemorrhages among academics). Your version of reality can only approximate mine; as Lily Tomlin says twenty-five centuries later, reality itself is just a collective hunch. Plato pointed out that if all truth is relative, that very statement, that nothing is absolutely true, could not be absolutely true, and attacked Protagoras for his materialism: the sophist earned as much as one hundred minae — about a thousand dollars — per student. Plato also accused him of dereliction of philosophical duties: Protagoras didn't want to find truth, Plato said; he just wanted to win arguments, by any means — an argument reinforced by the sharpsterism of Protagoras's contracts conundrum:

Bright strikes a bargain with his Contracts tutor, Professor Bart Vader. Bright will pay Vader for his instruction once Bright wins his first case. Their studies go on. One day, Vader declares that he has taught Bright all he knows and that Bright now owes him his fee. As Bright has not yet won his first case at bar, he refuses to pay.

Seeking to teach his pupil a graduation lesson, Vader files suit. Bright answers with a motion for nonsuit (no case to answer), claiming that because he is still willing to perform his part of the bargain, Vader cannot demonstrate a cause of action. There has been no breach of contract: Bright has not argued, let alone won, his first case.

Feeling his trap spring, Vader replies that, even so, he cannot lose: if Bright wins *this* case, he must pay Vader under the terms of the contract. If Bright loses the case, he must pay Vader because the court tells him to.

Bright, no dimwit, is prepared for this argument, and counters that it is he who cannot lose. If the court finds against him, the contract says he doesn't have to pay: he will not yet have won his first case. If the court finds in his favor, he can postpone payment because the judge will have freed him of that obligation.

If you attempt to reduce the problem to a legal syllogism, you get only as far as a contradiction:

- If A wins the case, he must pay B (because the contract says so).
- If A wins the case, he need not pay B (because the court says so).

That contradiction would seem to support a finding of nonsuit. Insofar as there can be no actual breach of contract until the court has rendered judgment (and then only if Bright succeeds: there is no breach unless Bright "wins his first case"), there is none at the time of argument. Ergo, there is no cause of action.

But must Bright then pay Vader anyway, under the terms of the contract? Bright might fall back on those terms and say that convincing the court to declare "no suit" is not "winning" a case — the case was never argued. *Black's Law Dictionary*, in fact, gives "nonsuit" as "a variety of termination of an action which does not adjudicate the issues on the merits."

In a declaration of nonsuit, judgment is rendered *against* the plaintiff, not in favor of the defendant. A nonsuit is not a victory but a draw. The defendant has parried but not counterthrust. Of course, the professor will reply that the contract says nothing about a decision on the merits of the case. A motion by itself is a separate trial of an issue, with a winner and a loser. If the court declares a nonsuit, Bright has won on that issue.

And what if Bright never becomes a lawyer or argues another case? Perhaps Vader should have foreseen such eventualities, but unless the court awards him his fee, he may well have given valuable consideration for no return. Bright will be unjustly enriched by Vader's tutoring.

Again, suppose the court decides to enter into the spirit of the dispute and decide the case on the merits, on the question of whether there was a breach of contract. There is no so-called "anticipatory breach," because Bright never refused to honor the contract on its terms. Technically, even on Vader's view there can be no breach until *after* the court has given judgment.

But insofar as Bright has said in his pleadings that he can't lose no matter whether the court finds for or against him (an admission that he *can* win?), might the court find a prospective breach, even as it tries that very issue?

Even analogy doesn't help much. Farmer delivers wheat flour to Baker. Baker agrees to pay for the flour with bagels he bakes using the flour. Farmer sues for payment while the bagels are in the oven. Although it is impossible for Baker to pay yet (just as Bright has not paid), it is not impossible for Farmer to sue (just as Vader has sued). Of course, the court can simply hold that Baker must pay once the bagels are crisp and brown. If he turns off the oven, we're back to unjust enrichment. (He gets wheat without paying for it.)

All discussion ends, it would seem, if we assume that whatever the *Vader* court says, its authority supersedes the terms of the contract. (You could say that by submitting their dispute to adjudication, Vader and Bright admit that fact.) If the court told Vader he would have to wait for payment, he would have to wait — never mind the semantics of whether Bright "won."

Perhaps the court's only choice is to tell Vader to give Bright the chance to perform — allow him three years to finish his law course,

then, if necessary, sue him for the fair market value of the lessons.*
Otherwise, it is forced to look outside the terms of the contract, to
the meaning of "winning" and "nonsuit," to what the parties
"intended," to what consideration was to flow from each side at what
time. Many of the cases discussed in this book make clear that, in
responding to the persistent economic and social after-shocks of the
Industrial Revolution — in order, really, to keep the peace — judges
have found such temptations irresistible, like quicksand or Venus
flytraps. Scrambling to adjust as the pace of human life rockets ahead,
they improvise according to the prevailing social and political climate.
The law of frustration, for example — as developed in the very midst
of the Revolution when fire claimed the music hall where Sims Reeves
was to sing, and a little later when an aging prince was finally to
be crowned king — is founded on something so nebulous and untouch-
able as what "the parties had in mind at the time of making the contract," regardless of what they committed to words.

In the Humber Ferryman's case, the courts established the footings
of the modern law of contract by implying a promise that the horse
would be delivered safely across the river. This reasonable implication has evolved into the voodoo ones of implied intentions, motivations, shades of meaning, and states of mind — developments which,
along with the expanding metaphysics of the doctrine of consideration and the now pervasive regulation by governments of contracts
(especially regarding employment and health care), have led to the
widespread belief in, as the title of the seminal work on the subject
says, *The Death of Contract*.

If "freedom to contract" remains a "paramount public policy," it
is a policy in search of a meaning. Probably the most regrettable
response has been "creative lawyering" — jumbling the dictionary

---

* When I discussed the Protagoras brain-teaser in my column in *The Lawyers Weekly*,
a reader in Vancouver pointed out that Bright could have the last laugh simply by
hiring a lawyer. The win or loss would go to that paid agent, and Bright would
not be "taking business away from real lawyers who are struggling to get by on a
measly $150 an hour." The Romans had a similar logic teaser: A crocodile grabs
a young man, challenging his mother, "I'll release him if you tell me his fate." The
mother says, "You won't release him." The crocodile is in a double bind, being obliged
to release the boy even if he *doesn't* release him.

and law reports on the precarious belay of a loophole. The feverish, sometimes apparently Talmudic reflex of many counsel to argue a case by torturing the English language (using principles unknown to conventional philology and grammar) has to be a prime cause for the popular view of lawyers as con men. Creative semantics is the clearest symptom of the profession's epidemic "Portia problem," an irresistible impulse to dress manipulation and perversion in the clothes of wisdom and sensitivity. Nowhere is this more rife than in contract law and negotiation.

It was really Swift who pulled no literary punches on this issue, his plain-spoken Gulliver characterizing lawyers as

> a society of men among us, bred up from their youth in the art of proving by words multiplied for the purpose, that *white* is *black* and *black* is *white*, according as they are paid. To this society all the rest of the people are slaves. . . . It is likewise to be observed, that this society hath a peculiar cant and jargon of their own, that no other mortal can understand, and wherein all their laws are written, which they take special care to multiply; whereby they have wholly confounded the very essence of truth and falsehood, or right and wrong; so that it will take thirty years to decide whether the field left me by my ancestors for six generations belongs to me, or to a stranger three hundred miles off.

But Shakespeare's more subtle approach has led many readers to find Portia, of *The Merchant of Venice*, a heroine in ways the Bard may well have not imagined. Indeed, English Court of Appeal Justice Charles Russell baldly came out of the closet in 1967 as a "Portia man," to use his own words, and if he had meant he enjoyed dressing up like a woman (who dressed up like a man — who, in Shakespeare's day, was already a man who dressed up like a woman . . . who dressed up like a man . . .), the consequences would have been considerably less tragic.

"I am a Portia man," Justice Russell said, unequivocally, but what he really meant was, "I am not a Lord Denning man." Lord Denning, he implied, was a "Bassanio man," an implication which seemed to be Lord Russell's way of agreeing with academics who wrote in law journals of Lord Denning's habit of dispensing "palm tree justice"

— of his penchant for singlehandedly (and *off*handedly) overturning entrenched law that he considered outdated, nonsensical or harsh. Or at least Lord Justice Russell implied that Lord Denning was practicing palm-tree justice in *Sydall v. Castings Ltd.*, a scarifying instance of the Portia problem as it concerned who would benefit under Francis Sydall's life insurance contract.

When he died in 1965, Sydall left five children, a wife he had separated from, and a lover, who was the mother of Sydall's youngest child, a baby girl named Yvette. After leaving his wife, Sydall had set up housekeeping with Yvette's mother.

His life had been insured for three hundred pounds by Castings Limited, where he had worked as a maintenance man. The company offered the insurance as an employment benefit, their goal being to help the neediest "relations" of an employee when the employee died. Castings, who had the right under the contract to decide which "relations" would receive the insurance money, wanted to name Yvette as a beneficiary. But following the old common law on illegitimacy and "descendants," Lord Russell and a majority of the Court of Appeal held that "descendant" — which was how the insurance contract defined "relation" — "is to be construed as descendant in the legitimate line." The company had negotiated the insurance contract and paid for it, but suddenly had no right, or "freedom," to define its terms.

Lord Denning dissented. "Because Yvette is illegitimate," he wrote,

> she is to be excluded from any benefit. She is on this view no "relation" of her father: nor is she "descended" from him. In the eye of the law, she is the daughter of nobody. She is related to nobody. She is an outcast and she is to be shut out from any part of her father's insurance benefit.

Lord Denning excoriated the common law view on "descendants" as Victorian, old-fashioned and vengeful, agreeing with the trial judge, who had found in favor of Yvette, that "anyone who turns over the pages of *Burke's Peerage*" would find British nobility claiming "illegitimate descent from the sovereigns of this country." He might have added, as one famous Victorian did, that if this was the way the law treated needy children, the law was "a ass."

Lord Russell rose directly to the challenge. He compared Lord Denning to Bassanio in *The Merchant of Venice*, Bassanio being the friend
of Antonio (who owes moneylender Shylock a large sum of money),
and intended of Portia. In the play's famous trial scene, Bassanio
pleads with Judge Balthazar (Portia in disguise, playing a practical
joke) not to make Antonio pay with a pound of his flesh in default
of his bond, even though Antonio has agreed to such a term.

"Wrest once the law to your authority," Bassanio begs
Balthazar/Portia. "To do a great right, do a little wrong." Lord
Russell quotes these words, and continues:

> But Portia retorted:
> It must not be, there is no power in Venice
> Can alter a decree established.
> 'Twill be recorded for a precedent,
> And many an error by the same example
> Will rush into the state. It cannot be.

And that was the point where Lord Russell ended the court's judgment in *Sydall v. Castings Ltd.*, declaring, "I am a Portia man."

Portia-in-drag technically refuses to let Antonio off the hook for
his pound of flesh, ostensibly because she does not dare establish a
precedent that would allow defaulting debtors to escape their obligations. Similarly, in Portian garb Lord Justice Russell is loathe to "open
the floodgates" to every marginal claim under insurance and other
contracts. (In passing, he also agrees with Mrs. Sydall's lawyer that
interpreting "descendants" to include children born out of wedlock
might cause "grave and embarrassing problems of tracing the content of the class.") He is not being heartless, his argument would have
it, but sensitive to the greater good: if he allows sympathy for Yvette
to guide his judgment, then every time someone dies his estate will
be "frittered away" by embarrassing litigation over who will benefit
as "descendants" and "beneficiaries."

This is perhaps a more percipient characterization of Portia than
Lord Justice Russell realizes. When you look closely at Portia's
character, she can seem to symbolize everything the common person
finds curious, and despicable, about the literal-mindedness of the
law. That women lawyers occasionally suffer being labelled "our

Portia" can only mean they haven't really investigated her character. She is legalistic in the most pejorative way. Her famous "contract judgment" is the speech of a jaded academic, a Machiavellian; it is founded in legal perversion and parody, Jew-baiting, and a perversely sexual pleasure in a clever deception, not on the obvious — and dramatically boring — fact that you cannot make a contract to kill somebody:

> Tarry a little, there is something else.
> This bond doth give thee here no jot of blood;
> The words expressly are "a pound of flesh."
> Take then thy bond, take thou thy pound of flesh,
> But in the cutting it, if thou dost shed
> One drop of Christian blood, thy lands and goods
> Are by the laws of Venice confiscate. . . .

With the aplomb of a practised show-off (and coquette), she appears to find for the despised moneylender, telling him that, yes, he may have his pound of flesh, but the bond says nothing about *blood*. This is the very worst sort of lawyering, the sort that led Ambrose Bierce to define "lawyer" as "one skilled in circumvention of the law." Bassanio urges on her a solution framed in equity and humanity — "To do a great right, do a little wrong." But to seem clever and crafty, and for the gratification of her ego, she insists on the *letter* of the law. Bassanio's view prevails only in a form twisted by Portia's perversity: she has done more than a little wrong to do a reasonable right. To an objective reader, her bored-little-rich-girl behavior recalls Bassanio's earlier observation,

> In law, what plea so tainted and corrupt
> But, being season'd with a gracious voice,
> Obscures the show of evil?

Surely Lord Russell does not really mean to be a "Portia man." He seems to forget that, unlike him, Portia finds for the defendant. Only in the matter of mincing words are they fellow travelers. At law, Portia is a savage parodist, twisting and hair-splitting to the last micron. (In a curious lapse of acuity some years later, Lord Denning remarked that his humanitarian approach to the law made *him* the Portia man.)

Then again, Lord Russell does end up denying six hundred dollars to a fatherless baby.

Sydall is reminiscent of a story about the ineffectiveness of air dryers in public toilets. The setting is a washroom in New York City, equipped with an air dryer fitted with the usual instructions. "1. Shake excess moisture from hands. 2. Press button. 3. Rub hands briskly under blower." Below number three a graffitist had added, "4. Wipe hands on pants."

Sometimes, as with both *Vader* and *Sydall*, the law leaves us no choice but to improvise. True, to avoid the prejudice of individual judges or the willfulness of the moment, to ward off the calamities of rushing to judgment, it must move cautiously, avoiding change for change's sake. But we must always consider the dangers of such conservatism, how it can be another name for bad old ideas; we must consider whether our law exists to enslave us to first principles or to serve us, reflecting and protecting our evolving humanity.

NOTES

CHAPTER ONE

Page 11: Swearing as casting a "provisional curse": see **Ashley Montagu**, *The Anatomy of Swearing* (Macmillan, 1976).

— Eliza says "bloody": New York *Times*, Apr. 14, 1914, as quoted in H.L. Mencken, *The American Language* (4th ed., 1937), Alfred A. Knopf, p. 311.

Page 12: Canton "chicken oath": *The King v. Ah Wooey* (1902), 8 C.C.C. 25 (B.C.S.C.).

— "Paper Oath": *R. v. Lai Ping* (1904), 11 B.C.L.R. 102 (C.A.).

— Refusing to swear allegiance to Queen: Canadian Press, 1986?

— Yoruba tribal oath: *State v. Fagemi, National Law Journal*, April 11, 1988, p. 59.

Page 13: Rooster blood case: *State v. Ching Xiong, National Law Journal*, Aug. 29, 1988, p. 59

— Blackstone on profanity: *Commentaries on the Laws of England* (1769), IV, 59.

— "Act more effectually to prevent cursing . . .": 19 Geo. 2, c. 21.

— Albert Haddock is no gentleman: *Rex v. Haddock* (1935, Methuen), *Uncommon Law* 18 (as reported by A.P. Herbert). When in 1722 a leather dresser was fined two shillings for each of 54 profane oaths and 160 curses, all uttered during just ten days, his conviction was overturned because the Crown had failed to prove that he was *not* a soldier (the court agreed that a man could be a leather dresser and soldier both), soldiers being entitled to that less onerous one-shilling levy. The appeal court also held that, as it was the man's right to know the charges he had to answer, the specific words of each of the 204 curses and oaths should have been set out in the indictment: *R. v. Sparling* (1722), 1 Str. 497. When, however, a man was charged in 1724 with saying only "God damn you" 150 times, the court rejected his argument that the curse had to be written out 150 separate times in the indictment (*R. v. Roberts* (1724), 1 Str. 608).

Even where there was no dispute about a curser's social station or the formal validity of an indictment, there might be technical argument about the rate of fine. When, in 1863, a mealman named John Scott was charged before the Buckinghamshire assizes with uttering twenty separate curses, he pleaded that, as he was charged on only *one* indictment with repeating the same *one* curse on *one* occasion (albeit twenty times on that one occasion) he should be fined at the single-curse rate of two shillings — instead of twenty times that, or two pounds. The justices held that, just like eggs and apples, twenty separate curses were twenty separate curses, two shillings *each (R. v. Scott* (1863), 4 B. & S. 368).

Page 14: *Rex v. Brough* (1748), 1 Wils. K.B. 244.
— *Nash v. Battersby* (1703), 2 Ld. Raym. 986.
— Norman ranking system to Cromwell: On the subject of swearing, oaths, blasphemy in general, see Ashley Montagu, *op. cit.*, note to page 7, and Jeffrey Miller, 1985 *Ontario Lawyers Weekly*, April 5 and 12, p.3.
— *R. v. Brodribb* (1816), 6 Carr. and P. 571.

Page 16: Humber Ferryman's Case: See, for example, Swan and Reiter, *Contracts: Cases, Notes, and Materials* (Butterworths, 1978), Chap. 2, p. 21.
— Sanctity of contract is a "paramount concern": *Printing and Numerical registering Co. v. Sampson* (1875), 19 Eq. 462, at 465-6.

Page 17: *Ruffolo v. Mulroney et al.*, unreported, June 28, 1988, Ontario Provincial Court.

Page 18: One story: from *To Juan at the Winter Solstice*.

CHAPTER TWO

Page 21: *B.C. Saw-Mill Co. v. Nettleship* (1868), 3 C.P. 499 at 508.
— Six centuries of litigation: This time span includes, of course, the days when "consideration" was not defined and played little *express* role in the common law.

Page 22: Trading in peppercorns: See, for example, Reay Tannahill, *Food in History* (Stein & Day, 1973), p. 189.
— Sir George Jessel's remark on tomtits: in *Couldery v. Bartrum* (1881), 19 Ch. 394 at 399. Again, were the boy in *Big* an adult, his payment of a mere twenty-five cents would be perfectly lawful, even though it seems absurdly little to pay to change everything in his life.

Page 23: *Hookes v. Swaine* (1663), 1 Sid. 151.
— Henchard's promise not to drink: Sobering and scraping bottom, Henchard prays in a chapel near the fairground that he be "strook dumb, blind and helpless" if he breaches the pledge. He rises to the top of the local community on the strength of the promise, only to come bounding back down for the breach of his marriage vows.
— A case something like Henchard's: *Hamer v. Sidway*, 27 N.E. 256 (1891, C.A.N.Y.)

Page 25: *White v. Bluett* (1853), 23 L.J.Ex. (N.S.) 36.
— A more recent precedent: *Talbott v. Stemmons*, 12 S.W. 297 (1889, C.A. Ky.).

Page 26: Running fathers: *Earl of March v. Pigot* (1771), 5 Burr. 2802. See also *Hampden v. Walsh*, a nineteenth-century case in which a court enforced a five-hundred-pound bet that certain demonstrations on a canal proved the earth was not flat, and *James v. Randall* (1774), 1 Cowp. 37 (enforcing a bet on the outcome of a lawsuit).

Page 28: Books by crooks: For a general discussion of the subject, see Sam Roberts, "Criminals, Authors and Criminal Authors," *New York Times Book Review*, March 22, 1987. p. 1.

Page 29: Major Rowlandson's case: I take the facts from both *Beresford v. Royal Insurance,* [1938] A.C. 586, and Lord Denning's personalized account in his *The Road to Justice* (Stevens, 1955), pp. 95 ff. A much more recent case demonstrates that this particular "public policy" can be twisted back on itself. In the United States, a woman was awarded $8 million in punitive damages when her husband's insurance company charged that he had committed suicide, which the husband's policy did not cover. Company staff doubted that they could prove suicide, but decided to "deny [payment of benefits] now and try for compromise later when she complains." While the benefits amounted only to $12,000, the insurance company's conduct cost it that, plus $150,000 for the woman's emotional suffering, plus the $8 million and legal costs. See Claire Bernstein, "Morality becoming factor in contracts," *The Globe and Mail* (Toronto), Jan. 21, 1985.

Page 30: *Northwestern Mutual v. Johnson,* 254 U.S. 96 (120).
— *Northwestern Mutual v. McCue,* 223 U.S. 234 (1911).

Page 31: *Farmer v. Russell* (1798), 1 Bof. and Pul. 296.

Page 32: A plaintiff named John Everet: The story seems to have originated with *The European Magazine,* May, 1787, p. 360, and was picked up by the French scholar Pothier in his *Law of Obligations.* The magazine, Pothier says, took it from "a copy of the proceedings . . . as found amongst the papers of a deceased attorney." In 1893, the editors of the *Law Quarterly Review* were able to track down the court documents and substantiate the extraordinary suit and its fallout (9 L.Q.R. 197), but it is the magazine which relates what eventually happened to the parties and lawyers. See also the note in the eleventh edition of *Lindley on Partnership* (1950) at 123, and the note at 20 Eq. 230, where Sir James Bacon refers to *Everet* during proceedings to settle a dispute between directors of a corporation.

Page 33: Fathers like turkeys in a shooting match: In *James v. Randall* (1774), 1 Cowp. 37, Lord Mansfield held, as well, that betting on the outcome of a lawsuit could be legal, as long as the bettors were not connected with the proceedings.
— *Pearce v. Brooks,* [1866] 1 Ex. 213.
— Edward Law, first Baron Ellenborough: Chief Justice of England from 1802 to 1818.
— *Bowry v. Bennet* (1808), 1 Camp. 348.

Page 34: An infant and a prostitute must have lodging: per Eyre, Ch.J., *Crisp v. Churchill* (1794), cited at 1 Bos. and Pul. 340 (in *Lloyd v. Johnson, infra.*).
— A madam can defeat a landlord even if she lies to him: *Feret v. Hill* (1854), 15 C.B. 207.
— Cleaning dresses and nightcaps: *Lloyd v. Johnson* (1798), 1 Bos. and P. 340.

Page 36: Past illicit intercourse: See, for example, *Sharon v. Sharon,* 8 P. 614 (1885).

— Wyoming sex-for-used-car case: (1984) *Ontario Lawyers Weekly*, August 3, p. 5.

— 1918 Rhode Island sex novelties case: *Manes Co. v. Glass*, 102 A. 964. Record supplied by the Supreme Court of Rhode Island.

Page 37: *Gardner v. Fulforde* (1667), 1 Lev. 204; *sub nom Gardner against Hulford* 2 Keb. 154. Poor Gardner's second try is reported at 2 Keb. 172.

— Action fails because middle name not spelled out: *Miscellany-at-Law*, (Stevens, 1958), p. 43. In 1844, Thomas Cox was acquitted of stealing "three eggs . . . of the goods and chattels of Samuel Harris" because the indictment had not specified that they were eggs of a guinea-fowl and not "adder's eggs, or some other species of eggs which cannot be the subject of larceny." The next day, the prosecutor in *Cox* crossed the courtroom before the same judge, to defend a man accused of committing bestiality "in and upon a certain animal called a bitch." No doubt full of confidence and smugly certain of the court's point of view, he cited *Cox* on the very point that had killed his case the day before: as in *Cox*, he asserted, the bestiality indictment did "not describe the animal with sufficient certainty," "bitch" by itself signifying perhaps a fox or otter bitch. While repeating what he had said in *Cox*, the judge anyway pronounced the bestiality indictment good. Probably he had not observed any otters traversing Salisbury Plain (1844, 1 Car. and K. 494, 495). Again, in 1823, Thomas Halloway was acquitted of "stealing a brass furnace" on the argument that, by the time he had brought the object within the jurisdiction of the court, he had broken it into pieces and it was no longer a furnace. It was a memorably lucky day for Halloway — on the same day in the same court, he was acquitted of pinching "two turkeys" because the indictment should have specified that the turkeys were dead. In a practice note to their report of Halloway's good fortune, Carrington and Payne, barristers of Lincoln's Inn, explain that live animals such as turkeys are in law *ferae naturae* (free-roaming beasts) and cannot be owned, let alone stolen. Ancillary to this, stealing the skin of a dog, they say, is a felony, but stealing the living dog is not, "dogs being considered in law of base [wild] nature." They add that regarding indictments for theft, counsel should remember that a man charged with stealing a "pair" of stockings was acquitted because the stockings did not match, and that another accused escaped punishment for stealing a duck because the converted bird was a *drake* (1 C. & P. 127).

— U.S. and Australian rewards cases: *Fitch v. Snedaker*, 38 N.Y. 248 (1868, C.A.); *Crown v. Clarke* (1927), 40 C.L.R. 227 (H.C. Aust.).

Page 38: The English aberration: *Williams v. Carwardine* (1833), 4 B.&Ald. 621.

Page 39: *Dagg v. Dagg* (1882), 7 P. 17.

Page 40: Egyptian marriage contract: *Hussein, Otherwise Blitz v. Hussein*, [1938] P. 159.

Page 41: Disciplining the little lady: See, for example, Lee Holcombe, *Wives and Property* (University of Toronto, 1983), especially at pp. 25-30.

— *Paynel's Case*, 1302: See note to (1554) 1 Dy. 106b; Rot. Parl. I, 140; and Pollock and Maitland, *The History of English Law Before the Time of Edward I* (Cambridge, 1923), Vol. 2, p. 396. Commoys' name is given variously as de Comeys, de Camoys, etc. I take the spelling from *Dyer's Reports*.

Page 42: Ann Parsons asks the court to ban her husband: Courtney Kenny, "Wife-Selling in England", *Parsons v. Parsons* (1929), 1945 L.Q.R. 494.

Page 43: The price for a wife: *Ibid.*

Page 44: A second wife-selling report in *The Times*: July 18, 1797.

— An example from the Wild West: (1973), 92 Law Notes 171.

Page 45: Tim Kowalke's cookie settlement: Associated Press, Sept. 9, 1979.

— English case from the 1950s: *Shaw v. Shaw*, [1954] 3 W.L.R. 265.

Page 46: Wallace Beery sued for child support: 224 P.2d 54, 56 (1950). See also *Sharon v. Sharon*, 8 P. 614 (1885, Cal. C.A.) (past illicit cohabitation).

— Maryland man pays on false pretenses: *Fiege v. Boehm*, 123 A.2d 316 (1956).

Page 47: 1892 Australian judgment on separation agreement: *Dunton v. Dunton* (1892), 18 Vict. L.R. 114.

CHAPTER THREE

Page 51: "The purchaser cannot be supposed" to buy garbage: *Gardiner v. Gray* (1815), 14 Camp. 144.

Page 52: The assizes of bread: Walton Hamilton, "The Ancient Maxim *Caveat Emptor*" (1931), 60 Yale L.J. 1133.

— John Brid's trapdoor: Reay Tannahill, *Food in History* (Stein & Day, 1973), pp. 200-201. Hamilton reports the trapdoor ruse as more widely practiced. General information about baking in the Middle Ages can also be found in Katie Stewart, *Cooking and Eating* (Hart-Davis, 1975), p. 56.

— Assizes of beer: Some of my information about ale-conning comes from an essay by Professor R.D. Connor, Professor Emeritus at the University of Manitoba, in *Ontario Lawyers Weekly*, October 4, 1985, p. 4. See also Hamilton, *op. cit.*

Page 53: Rotten meat, sandy wheat: Hamilton, 1139 ff.

— A credible theory about "ducking-stool": For this etymology, see the Oxford English Dictionary, and note that the ducking-stool was also called a "tumbrel," from the French *tombereau*, "a dung cart." The fact that these were used to transport refuse for dumping in ponds and rivers would suggest offenders sentenced to ducking may have been dipped in muck heaps or especially polluted water.

Page 54: *James v. Morgan*: The precise date of the case is disputed, but is set approximately at the early 1600s: 1 Keb. 569, 1 Lev. 111.

— 4,294 . . . I owe the arithmetic here to Mr. Robert Douglas of Ottawa, who was afflicted with mine in my column in *Lawyers Weekly* and wrote to correct me.

— A similar but even more awesome case: *Thornburgh v. Whitacre* (1705), 3 Salk. 97; *sub nom. Thornborow*, 2 Ld. Raym 1164; *sub nom. Thornborough* (1704), 6 Mod. 305. As Salkeld was Whitacre's counsel, I have accepted his spelling of the plaintiff's name. The arithmetic is mine, and therefore not really reliable.

Page 55: Rent of one-third penny: *Edgecombe v. Burnaford* (1729), Jones (T) 139.

— *Marsham v. Buller* (1618), 2 Roll. Rep. 19. In paraphrasing and quoting from the case, I have translated from law French, in this instance only a slightly adulterated form of that Norman contribution to Anglo-American law, used from about the twelfth through sixteenth centuries in English courts: "Richardson in arrest de judgment dit, que le damage que le jury done al plaintiff doit estre valuable, & nest ascun tiel coyne come half a farthing." In the original, Justice Dodridge's words read: "Vestre purse est plein, mes si vous estes al Oxon, vous aves un draught de beer pur half a farthing, Haughton vous poyes aver fieri fascias, and levy half a farthing pur un egg." (An influential Norwich judge of the day was called Sir Robert *Houghton*, but whether he had any doings in pub disputes is doubtful.)

Page 56: One "jungle" theory: Loren Eiseley, "The Real Secret of Piltdown," in *The Immense Journey* (Random House, 1955).

Page 57: Picking an empty pocket: See *R. v. Ring* (1892), 17 Cox 491, overturning *R. v. Collins* (1864), 10 L.T. 581.

— American authority on laxative jokes: *State v. Monroe*, 28 S.E. 547 (1897, S.C. North Carolina). Although Monroe did not know what the pranksters wanted to do with the laxative (croton oil), he was aware that they had once dosed the intended victim with quinine in lemonade. He therefore "knew or had every reason to believe, and did believe, that it was intended for [the victim] or some other person by way of a trick or joke."

— Adulterated coffee and cocoa: Tannahill, *op. cit.*, pp. 344 ff.

— Doing business on the Lord's day: Compare *James Bagg's Case* (1615), 11 Co. Rep. 93b, discussed in Chapter Four.

Page 58: *The Law Journal: Bullen v. Ward* (1905), 74 L.J. (K.B.).

Page 59: Ice cream is not meat: *Slater v. Evans*, [1916] 2 K.B. 124.

Page 60: Novas won't go in South America, Pepsi for corpses: From an Associated Press story quoting Joseph Lurie's "eighteen-page study called 'America, Globally Deaf and Mute.'"

— Japanenglish on food products: *The Toronto Star*, Dec. 26, 1984, p. D29.

Page 61: Arizona District Court: *Coca-Cola Co. of America v. Koke Co. of America*, 235 F. 908 (1919).

— Arizona Circuit Court: 255 F. 894.

Page 62: *Coca-Cola Co. of America v. Gay-Ola Co.*, 200 F. 720 (1912). *U.S v. Forty Barrels and Twenty Kegs of Coca-Cola* (241 U.S. 265), a prosecution contesting Coca-Cola's "fitness" under federal law, raised similar issues. The government argued that, given there was "no coca and little cola" in the drink, and that caffeine might be deleterious to human health, Coke was an unlawful "adulterated" substance.

   — U.S. Circuit Court of Appeals on Coke versus Koke: *Coca-Cola Co. of America v. Koke Co. of America*, 254 U.S. 143 (1920).

Page 64: *Bile Bean Manufacturing Co. v. Davidson*, [1906] Sessions Cas. 1181 (Scotland). A U.S. case similar in some ways to *Bile Bean*, and one referred to in the *Koke* cases, is *Worden v. California Fig Syrup Co.*, 187 U.S. 516 (1902).

Page 66: Charles Forde as mere puffery: For more on the distinction between a puff and a contractual promise, see Chapter Six.

   — Daniel M'Naghten: *M'Naghten's Case* (1843), 10 Cl. & Fin. 200. With the John Hinckley case as its point of reference (Hinckley was found not guilty by reason of insanity in the shooting of President Ronald Reagan and members of his entourage), *The Insanity Defense* by Lincoln Caplan (Dell, 1987) provides a concise and timely review of problems in the U.S. caused, or thought to be caused, by allowing defendants in criminal cases to plead mental impairment. See also Shirley Frondorf, *The Death of a Jewish American Princess* (Villard, 1988) and Mike Weiss, *Double Play* (Addison-Wesley, 1984).

Page 67: Remoteness of damages in breach of contract: The classic statement is *Hadley v. Baxendale* (1854), 156 E.R. 145.

   — *Jarvis v. Swans Tours*, [1973] 1 All E.R. 71. I owe the insight about the correlation between Jarvis's distress damages and his "lost salary" to Swan and Reiter, *op. cit.*, Chap. 1, p. 135.

Page 69: *Donoghue v. Stevenson*, [1932] A.C. 562. I repeat a caution from the literature about the case: insofar as the dispute never went to trial, the snail should properly be called an "alleged snail."

Page 70: Mrs. Donoghue settles for £100: R.F.V. Heuston, "*Donoghue v. Stevenson* in Retrospect" (1957), 20 Mod. Law Rev. 1.

Page 71: An Irish case about crabs: *Wallis v. Russell*, [1902] 2 I.R. 585.

Page 72: Ellen surprisingly well-versed in *Sale of Goods Act:* Maurice Healey, *The Old Munster Circuit*, 1939, p. 209. Sir Peter O'Brien was famous for his lisp and became known, cruelly, as "Sir Pether." Maurice Healey's "eyewitness account" of the *Wallis* trial does not spare his lordship: "You thaid that . . . In thothe very wordth? . . . Remarkable the strideth education is making," etc.

Page 74: Applesauce unfit for dessert: *Martel v. Duffy-Mott*, 166 N.W.2d 541 (1969).

Page 75: Lord Ellenborough has a taste for turbot: Reported in Stephen Tumim, *Great Legal Disasters* (Arthur Barker, 1983), p. 57.

CHAPTER FOUR

Page 80: Coke bride, Pepsi groom: See *Ontario Lawyers Weekly*, Sept. 13, 1985.

   — Jury rules against IBM: See, e.g., Robert Ellis Smith, *Workrights*, Dutton, 1983.

— *Denham v. Patrick* (1910), 20 O.L.R. 347.

Page 82: *James Bagg's Case* (1615), 11 Co. Rep. 93b.

Page 84: Don't leave home without protection: *Lawyers Weekly*, March 4, 1988.

— Mutant of Omaha case: *Mutual of Omaha v. Novak*, 648 F. Supp. 905 (U.S.D.C.); aff'd 775 F. 2d 147 (1985, U.S.C.A.), 836 F.2d 397 (8th Cir., 1987).

— Lardashe case: *Jordache Ent. v. Hogg Wyld*, 828 F.2d 1482 (10th Cir., 1987).

— *Burgess v. Burgess* (1853), 3 De G.M. & G. 896.

Page 85: Contracts among relatives: See, for example, *Jones v. Padavatton*, [1969] 2 All E.R. 616, concerning a mother's promise to support and house her daughter; *Simpkins v. Pays* in Chapter Six; and Chapter Two.

— *Burgess* was soon overturned: See *Schweitzer v. Atkins* (1867), 37 Ch. 847, in which the evidence showed that the plaintiff, an analytical chemist, had made a great success of his cocoa, a personal invention he called "Schweitzer's cocoatina, or anti-dyspeptic cocoa, registered." The deendant Atkins, a relative of Carl's wife, had helped Carl market Cocoatina, and when Atkins wanted to go into business for himself, kindly Carl had lent him the money to do it. With Carl Schweitzer bankrolling him, Atkins set up a partnership with an *Otto* Schweitzer, and together they began selling their own cocoa concoction, "Otto Schweitzer, Atkins & Co.'s cacaotine, registered." Its packaging, not to mention its name, betrayed a marked resemblance to that of Carl Schweitzer's Cocoatina, although, according to *The Law Reports*, purchasers of Cacaotine got a great deal more drink-mix for their money. As well, the Cacaotine label included a description of the product "but in small print," and the directions for use of each product "were quite different."

Sir Richard Malins, Vice-Chancellor of the High Court of Chancery, found that the buyer would easily confuse Atkins' cocoa for old Carl's, not reading the fine print until she got the package home. And the name of Atkins' cocoa was so clumsy, Vice-Chancellor Malins decided, that its only purpose could have been to confuse, especially considering that the suffix "-tine" was "wholly unmeaning and could only have been adopted because of its similarity" to the "-tina" used by Carl Schweitzer. His lordship ruled that *Burgess* did not apply because, in that case, William Burgess's anchovy sauce and its label were substantially different from his father's sauce and label — a distinction that does not exactly leap out of the facts in that case. Clearly, the vice-chancellor was simply uncomfortable with how close *Burgess* came to sanctioning commercial theft.

Page 86: Albert Hall Orchestra: *Hall of Arts and Sciences v. Hall* (1934), 50 T.L.R. 518.

— *Landa v. Greenberg* (1908), 24 T.L.R. 441.

Page 87: *Hines v. Winnick*, [1947] 1 Ch. 708.

Page 88: The Canadian tax scene; sarcasm and shrewd "avoidance" ruses: Paul Malvern and George Vandenberg, *Fighting Back* (Methuen, 1984).

Page 89: All writer's costs deductible: *Haddock v. Board of Inland Revenue* (1935), *Uncommon Law* (Methuen) 231.

— Court steno sues for "wear and tear of the plant": *Norman v. Golder (Inspector of Taxes)* (1944), 114 L.J. K.B. 108.

Page 90: Embezzlement not tax deductible: *Commissioner of Internal Revenue v. Wilcox*, 327 U.S. 404 (1946).

— Suit bonus: *Wilkins v. Rogerson*, [1961] Ch. 133.

— *Minister of Revenue v. Eldridge*, [1965] 1 Ex. C.R. 758. See also "Prostitutes demonstrate against U.K. tax collector," *The Globe and Mail* (Toronto, from Canadian Press story), Nov. 8, 1984, p. 13, and No. 275 v. M.N.R. (1955), 13 T.A.B. Cases, 279 (Canada).

Page 92: Bad things happen to priest: Reuter, July 11, 1986.

— Man beaten to death with own arm: "Welland woman pleads guilty to manslaughter," *The Globe and Mail* (Toronto, from a Canadian Press story), Sept. 27, 1978.

— Complexes "stamped out": Reuter, May 16, 1979, Dreux, France. The man's "complexes" included "obsessional fears" and difficulty in socializing, especially with women.

Page 93: *Vann v. Ionta*, 284 N.Y.S. 278 (1935); *The Globe and Mail*, Dec. 7, 1935.

Page 94: *Koistinen v. American Export Lines*, 83 N.Y.S.2d 197 (1948).

Page 95: Du Parcq L.J. in coke-worker case: *Gibby v. East Grinstead Gas and Water Co.* (1944), 170 L.T. 250 at 253.

— Rotten privy case: *Rush v. Commercial Realty Co.*, 145 A. 476 (1929).

— Creed murder case: *R. v. Smith*, [1959] 2 Q.B. 35.

Page 96: Courts as guardians of sailors: This conveniently ignored the fact that the "guardian" had often proved to be about as tender as the North Sea. Supposedly to protect a ship's captain from the extortionate whims of the crew when he was at their mercy under sail, the common law also said that "when the freight is lost, the wages are also lost." In effect this meant that if during a voyage a captain promised to pay a sailor a bonus for more work than he had been hired to perform, the law would not hold the captain to his word. When a sailor sued on such a bargain in 1791 (the ship having evidently encountered rough weather or difficult navigation problems), Lord Kenyon told him that if the courts enforced it, sailors "would in many cases suffer a ship to sink, unless the captain would pay any extravagant demand they might think proper to make." *Harris v. Watson* (1791), Peake 102.

In 1809, in the leading case of *Stilk v. Myrick* (1809), 2 Camp. 317, Lord Ellenborough applied technical contract law to Lord Kenyon's public policy rationale. There was no consideration for such agreements, he said. Before they set sail, seamen had bargained to provide any services necessary during the voyage, no matter what dangers came up, including mutiny, desertion, and shipwreck.

CHAPTER FIVE

Page 99: Coke on "mortgage": *Institutes* (1628), 205.

Page 100: A really dead hand does the deed: *Custodes v. Howell Gwinn* (1652), Sty. 362.

Page 101ff.: The British-North America tenure system: The *Encyclopedia Britannica*, 1972, contains some very readable articles. My examples of serjeanty, and the Somersetshire widow's penance, come from the delightful *Fragmenta Antiquitatis, Or, Antient Tenures of Land, and Jocular Customs of Some Manors* by Josiah Beckwith. The edition of 1784 includes entertaining notes.

Page 102: Liens on Pony Express horses: *U.S. v. Barney*, 3 Hall's L.J. 128 (1810).
— Murderous mailman: *U.S. v. Kirby*, 74 U.S. 482 (1868).

Page 103: *Larson v. St. Francis Hotel*, 188 P.2d 513 (1948).
— *Sayers v. Harlow Urban District Council*, [1958] 2 All E.R. 342.

Page 104: Contract for non-existent concert-hall: See *Taylor v. Caldwell*, Chapter Seven.

Page 105: Frustrating coronation: *Krell v. Henry*, [1903] 2 K.B. 740.
— Other coronation cases: cf. *Herne Bay Steamboat Co. v. Hutton*, in the same volume as *Krell*, at 683. *Chandler v. Webster*, [1904] 1 K.B. 493, is an example of how the rule could work unjustly (even among honest bargainers).

Page 106: Sense eventually prevails: *Fibrosa Spolka Akeyjna v. Fairbairn, Lawson, Combe, Barbouk Ltd.* [1943] A.C. 32.
— Gazumping: Rosten's remark is from a letter to me, dated October 7, 1985. See also *Solicitor's Journal*, Feb. 11, 1972, 110 and *Damm v. Damm* (1794), 234 E.G. 365.
— Is a parking lot a bawdy house?: *R. v. Pierce and Golloher* (1982), 37 O.R. 2d 721.

CHAPTER SIX

Page 111: One-sided contract, two-sided page: See Stanley Jackson, *Laughter at Law* (Arthur Barker, 1961), p. 10.
— County court judge on mysterious contracts among strangers: (1944), 94 L.J. News 367. In *Miscellany-At-Law*, p. 209, note 1, Robert Megarry says that the sentiment originated with Judge Sir Gerald Hurst.

Page 112: Offer and acceptance in retail sales: The leading case, and the one on non-prescription drugs, is *Pharmaceutical Society of Great Britain v. Boots Cash Chemists*, [1953] 1 Q.B. 401 (C.A.).

Page 113: *Carlill v. Carbolic Smoke Ball Co.*, [1893] 1 Q.B. 256 (C.A.).

Page 115: Trash hauling in Tulsa: *AAA...Inc. v. Southwestern Bell*, 373 P.2d 31 (1962).

Page 116: *Fred Harvey v. Corporation Commission*, 229 P. 428 (1924).

Page 117: *U.S. v. One Box of Tobacco*, 190 F. 731 (1911).

— Bank head not a genocidal gambler: Canadian Press, June 7, 1982.

— Lifetone alarms case: *Sherwood v. Leach*, 409 P.2d 160 (1965, S.C. Wash.).

Page 118: *The Dark Side of the Marketplace* (Prentice-Hall, 1968), p. 74.

Page 119: Lovers are gamblers: "Half Jackpot Given to Lover of Lottery Winner," *The Globe and Mail*, October 3, 1985.

— Landlady and lodger are partners: *Simpkins v. Pays*, [1955] 3 All E.R. 10.

Page 120: *Quiamco v. Gaspar*, unreported, April 19, 1984, British Columbia Supreme Court; see "Lawyers can't lose in lottery litigation," Robert Frater, *Ontario Lawyers Weekly*, Sept. 6, 1985.

— *Pando v. Fernandez*, 485 N.Y.S. (2d) 162 (1984).

Page 122: Contract bridge is not skill-testing: *R. v. Ross*, [1969] 70 D.L.R.(2d) 606 (S.C.C.).

— Peeling potatoes is not skill-testing: *R. v. Wallace* (1954), 109 C.C.C. 351. Because the potato peelers were drawn by lot (there were 20 of them, competing for ten automobiles in a charity benefit "jamboree"), the Alberta Supreme Court held that they "might well be without any real skill in paring a potato, and the cars would go to the ten least unskilful or inefficient of the twenty so chosen, or . . ., if any of the twenty should prove skilful, they were chosen as contestants by chance." This of course ignores the fact that a task can be "skill-testing" apart from the abilities (or disabilities) of those who perform it.

Page 123: Estimating barrel velocity *is* skill-testing: *R. v. Roe* [1949] 2 D.L.R. 785 (S.C.C.).

— *Ranger v. Herbert A. Watts Ltd.*, [1970] 10 D.L.R.(3d) 395; aff'd (1971) 29 D.L.R.(3d) 650.

Page 128: Contest advisory quoted from "Beatrice Dream Kitchen Sweepstakes," 1984.

Page 129: Vacuum-cleaner case: *Trans-Canada Credit Corp. v. Zaluski* (1969), 5 D.L.R.(3d) 702 (Ont. Co. Ct.).

Page 131: Dancing nurse: *Gaertner v. Fiesta Dance Studios* (1972), 32 D.L.R.(3d) 639 (B.C.S.C.).

Page 132: Another dancing nurse: *Grieshammer v. Ungerer* (1958), 14 D.L.R.(2d) 599.

— *Lloyds Bank v. Bundy*, [1974] 3 All E.R. 757 (C.A.).

Page 134: A foolish bargain is a bargain all the same: And it may receive legal sanction by juries as well as judges, even if "twelve men good and true" have to jumble the dictionary to do it. (It is every person's right, after all, to be tried by a jury of his foolish peers!) Just a few years ago, as part of what was evidently a promotion stunt, the owner of a saloon in Tallahassee, Florida, offered a prize of $25 to any patron wearing a t-shirt "bearing a date prior to 1977," with a bonus of five dollars for every year preceding 1976. A psychology professor claimed the prize with a shirt she purchased, it would seem, in 1978, if not later: "The Tower of London," the shirt proclaimed, "1078-1978." The date the shirt bore, the woman asserted, met the contest criteria by 899 years. The saloon-keeper refused payment. Newspaper accounts don't say, but his defense was probably that, by "bearing a date prior to," he meant a t-shirt purchased in 1976 or earlier. But a jury awarded the psychologist $4,515 plus costs. See *Ontario Lawyers Weekly*, July 29, 1983, where the damages are given as $4,490. My own shaky math suggests that someone forgot to add in the initial $25: $25 + (five dollars × 898 years prior to 1976) = $4,515. Bets as contracts are discussed in Chapter Two.

CHAPTER SEVEN

Page 137: Typical essay on J.D. Salinger: See Henry Anatole Grunwald (ed.), *Salinger* (Harper and Row, 1962), especially Grunwald's introduction.
— *Salinger v. Random House:* 650 F.Supp. 413 (S.D.N.Y., 1986); rev'd 811 F.2d 90 (C.A. 2nd Cir., 1987), reh'g denied, 818 F.2d 252. See also *New York Times Book Review*, Nov. 1, 1987, page 1.

Page 139: Gerald Ford sues *The Nation: Harper and Row v. Nation Enterprises*, 105 S.Ct. 2218 (1985).

Page 141: Carol Rinzler on Salinger case: *Publishers Weekly*, April 24, 1987, p. 21.
— *In Search of J.D. Salinger:* Reviewed by Mordecai Richler in the *New York Times Book Review*, June 5, 1988.
— *Snow v. The Eaton Centre* (1982), 70 C.P.R.(2d) 105.

Page 142: William Miller on art in shopping malls: *The Globe and Mail* (Toronto), June 1, 1987, p. 6.

Page 143: *Cummins v. Bond,* [1927] 1 Ch. 167.
— Luke on Cleophas: Luke 24:18. See also *Harper's Bible Dictionary*, 1973.

Page 145: The controversial life and times of Joe Bob Briggs: *Joe Bob Goes to the Drive-In* (Delacorte, 1987). Calvin Trillin, *The New Yorker*, Dec. 22, 1986, pp. 73-88.

Page 150: Bette Davis and specific performance: *Warner Bros. v. Nelson*, [1937] 1 K.B. 209.
— *Primo basso* as caged bird: *De Rivafinoli v. Corsetti*, 4 Paige 264 (1833).

Page 151: Corbin on *De Rivafinoli: Corbin on Contracts*, 1964, Vol. 5A, s. 1204, p. 400.
— Music hall burns down: *Taylor v. Caldwell* (1863), 8 L.T. 356.

Page 152: Pollock on Sims Reeves (1822-1900): *For My Grandson* (John Murray, 1933), p. 113.

Page 153: Was Gio Hernandez Lee Iacocca's agent?: *Hernandez v. Bantam Books*, S.C.N.Y. 14505/1985, June 19 and July 24, 1985. And see Peter Wyden, *The Unknown Iacocca* (William Morrow, 1987), Chapter 12 and following.

Page 154: Cohn says $5,000 no better than a tip: Wyden, *op. cit.*

Page 155: *Edwards v. Tracy Starr's* (1985), 33 Alta. L.R. (2d) 115.

CHAPTER EIGHT

Page 160: Only God can make perfect noses: *Sullivan v. O'Connor*, 296 N.E.2d 183 (1973, S.C. Mass.).

— *Hawkins v. McGee* 146 A. 641 (1929, S.C.N.H.).

— Hand grew hair: See, e.g., Howard O. Hunter, *The Modern Law of Contracts* (Warren, Gorham, Lamont, 1986), s. 4.03[4], n. 68.

Page 161: *Lopus v. Chandelor (sub. nom. Chandelor v. Lopus)* (1603), Cro. Jac. 4, 2 Rolle Rep. 5, Dyer, 75a. According to documents discovered in the 1890s by Professor J.H. Beale, the case reported in Dyer is Lopus's *second* attempt, when he pleaded that Chandelor had "warranted" the stone to be a bezoar. (At first instance, the court had dismissed the action because Lopus had not "averred" this in his pleadings.) See 8 Harv. L.R. 282-3 (1894), 7 Harv. L.R. 213 (1893), and 1 Harv. L.R. 191 (1887). In the three centuries preceding Professor Beale's discovery, the outcome of *Chandelor* had been murky. In a 1618 suit dealing with the fraudulent sale of jewelry, plaintiff's counsel evidently cited it, remarking that because Chandelor had deliberately misrepresented the stone, Lopus ultimately succeeded: "As in *Chandelor v. Lopus*, adjudged in this Court . . . , where one sells a Bezar stone, *sciens* [knowing] that it was counterfeit, and he did not warrant it: yet because that it was '*sciens*' the plaintiff had judgment" (*Southern v. How*, Cro. Jac. 468). The confusion in the reports probably reflects rife judicial confusion: *Croke's Reports* have Lopus suing for £100; the manuscript uncovered by Prof. Beale has him suing for £200.

Page 162: Hawkinses settle; McGee's insurers won't indemnify him: See, e.g., Swann and Reiter, *Contracts: Cases, Notes and Materials* (Butterworths, 1978), p. 1-67.

Page 163: Lord Mansfield's attack on consideration doctrine: *Pillans v. Van Mierop* (1765), 3 Burr. 1664, at 1669-70.

Page 164: *The Bank of England v. Boggs: The Times* (London), Nov. 2, 1986 and magazine for that date; Jan. 6, 14, 26; Apr. 9; May 5; Nov. 1, 24, 27, 29, all 1987. Lawrence Weschler published a profile of Boggs, including a description of the trial and events leading to it, in *The New Yorker*, Jan. 18 and 25, 1988.

Page 166: "Moron in a hurry" standard: See *Morning Star Co-op. Soc. v. Express Newspapers*, [1979] F.S.R. 113 at 117.

Page 167: Protagoras's conundrum: See, e.g., Cameron Harvey, *Legal Wit and Whimsy* (Methuen, 1988), p. 124.

Page 170n.: Roman crocodile conundrum: R.G. Hamilton, *All Jangle and Riot* (Professional Books, 1986), p. 2. The reader's solution to the Protagoras brain-teaser was forwarded to me by Brad Daisley, Vancouver bureau chief for *Lawyers Weekly*. The quoted words are his.

Page 170: Grant Gilmore, *The Death of Contract* (Ohio State, 1974).

Page 171: Swift, *Gulliver's Travels*, Part IV, Chapter 5.

— Lord Russell declares he is a Portia man: *Sydall v. Castings Ltd.,* [1967] 1 Q.B. 301 (C.A.). "Our Portia," by the way, is the affectionate name given to Phillida Erskine-Brown — née Trant — by her colleague and mentor, Rumpole of the Bailey, who is enough of a Shakespeare scholar to know better.

Page 174: Bierce on "lawyer": *The Devil's Dictionary*, 1957.

— Lord Denning declares *he* is a Portia man: *The Discipline of Law* (Butterworths, 1979), p. 31.

TABLE OF CASES